THE
BANKRUPTCY OF INDIA

THE BANKRUPTCY OF INDIA

AN ENQUIRY INTO THE ADMINISTRATION OF INDIA UNDER THE CROWN

H. M. HYNDMAN

GYAN

Published by

Gyan Publishing House
5, Ansari Road
Daryaganj, New Delhi-110002
Phone: 011-47034999, 9811692060
E-mail: books@gyanbooks.com

Distribution Network
gyanbooks.com
India, USA, Canada, UK, Australia

ISBN: 978-93-7014-202-2 (PB)

First Published, 1885

2nd Impression 2025

Printed at: Gyan Press, Delhi.

THE BANKRUPTCY OF INDIA

Arthur H. M. HYNDMAN

THE

BANKRUPTCY OF INDIA.

An Enquiry into the Administration of India under the Crown.

INCLUDING

A CHAPTER ON THE SILVER QUESTION.

BY

H. M. HYNDMAN,

AUTHOR OF "ENGLAND FOR ALL," "THE HISTORICAL BASIS OF SOCIALISM IN ENGLAND," ETC.

LONDON:
SWAN SONNENSCHEIN, LOWREY & CO.,
PATERNOSTER SQUARE.

1886.

PREFACE.

THE three chapters in this little book headed respectively, "The Condition of India," "Controversy," and "Bleeding to Death," appeared as papers in the *Nineteenth Century*, between the end of the year 1878 and the beginning of 1880. The title, "The Bankruptcy of India," was suggested by the editor of that Review, Mr. James Knowles. These articles are now reprinted almost as they then stood. I have altered neither the arguments nor the figures, because to have done so would have changed the controversial position as against my opponents, Sir John Strachey, Sir Erskine Perry, Mr. John Morley, and Mr. F. Danvers. Unfortunately for India, no reform of any importance has since been made, and my contentions remain wholly unshaken with regard to the period which I then dealt with. The "Introduction," the chapter headed "Continued Neglect," and the chapter on "The Silver Question," have been written for this volume.

It is pleasing to me to recall the fact, that after many years of study devoted to Indian matters, my first opportunity for calling attention to what has always seemed to me the most important point in connection with our rule, was given me in the *Pall Mall Gazette*, then edited by my old friend, and enemy, Mr. Frederick Greenwood. A series of letters, entitled "Our Greatest Danger in India," appeared in that newspaper signed "H." In one of them I criticised the administration of the Public Works Department in India very severely. A Committee of the House of Commons was then sitting to inquire into the management of that very department. The late Mr. Henry Fawcett, a member of the Committee, who curiously enough had been my lecturer in Political Economy at Cambridge, wrote to Mr. Greenwood and asked that "H" should offer himself as a witness before the Committee, seeing that the contributor who wrote over that initial evidently knew more about the subject than most of the officials who had been examined. As I had never been in India, and had acquired my information almost entirely from Blue Books and other official records, I, of course, declined to come forward; and I only mention this now because it enforces the view which I urge in the following pages,—that there is already plenty of evidence about India to enable any industrious man to master the facts, and to meet the arguments of the official apologists successfully. Shortly afterwards Mr. Knowles opened the pages of the *Nineteenth Century* to my articles.

I can only hope that, whatever defects of matter or style may be found in this little volume, it may have some effect in directing public attention to the irremediable mischief which must be done in India by a continuance of our present system. I am well aware that in pointing to manifest decay and hopeless misery, where writers of the highest official and literary distinction tell us to observe only improvement and prosperity, I run the risk of being accused of presumption and ignorance. But I have at least done my best to read all that they have written, and nine-tenths of my arguments are drawn from their own works and reports. To take the optimist view of the Indian problem is far more pleasant, as it is assuredly more profitable, than to state disagreeable truths in plain language.

I am, however, firmly convinced that in India we are working up to a hideous economical catastrophe, beside which the great Irish Famine of 1847 will seem mere child's play. What is more, I believe that no unprejudiced man can read through the official evidence summarised in this volume without coming to the same conclusion. With these few words, therefore, I leave the work to the judgment of the public.

H. M. H.

10, Devonshire Street,
Portland Place,
London, W.

CONTENTS.

	PAGE
INTRODUCTION - - - - - - - - -	1
I. THE CONDITION OF INDIA - - - - - -	35
II. CONTROVERSY - - - - - - - - -	78
III. BLEEDING TO DEATH - - - - - - -	115
IV. CONTINUED NEGLECT - - - - - - -	154
V. THE SILVER QUESTION - - - - - - -	198

INTRODUCTION.

When Englishmen speak and write of the history of India, they too often forget what an insignificant portion of that history the record of our conquest and domination really forms. Three thousand years ago the nations of India were a collection of wealthy, and, in a sense, highly-civilised peoples, with at least one great language, with an elaborate code of laws and social regulations, possessed of exquisite artistic taste and beautiful manufactures of many kinds, and endowed with religious ideas and philosophic thoughts which have greatly—we still scarcely know how greatly—influenced the development of the most progressive races of the West. Perhaps the noblest teacher and moralist that ever lived, Sakya Mouni, was a Hindoo; the Code of Menu, of the ninth century before our era, is still as essential a study for the jurist as the Laws of the Twelve Tables or the Institutes of Justinian; the philosophers of India held their own even with men who had argued with Aristotle and Alexander; Akbar, the Mahommedan, was the greatest monarch that ever ruled the East; while even in later times nations over whom we hold supremacy have proved that they have among them no unworthy descendants of the authors of the

Vedas and the Mahabharat, of the architects of the Taj Mahal or Beejapore, of Toder Mull and Nana Furvana, of Baber and Hyder Ali. Yet to read nine-tenths of what has been written on Indian life and administration of late years by Anglo-Indian officials, we should almost believe that civilised government in India began with the English Raj; that, but for our intervention, anarchy and ignorance would have been striving for mastery in the benighted country which we have been appointed by Providence to rescue from its unhappy fate; and that to hand over the direct government to a much greater degree to the ablest natives would be gross injustice to the people of India.

There is little basis for such contentions as these, though they find so much favour with our Indian bureaucracy. It is safe to say, for example, that never at any period was the condition of India more anarchical than that of France, Germany, the Low Countries, and Italy during a great portion of the Middle Ages. Thugs and dacoits were at no time more dangerous or more cruel than the bands of écorcheurs, robbers, and freebooters who roamed at will through some of the finest regions of Europe. The exactions of the feudal chieftains were in many cases worse than the heaviest demands made by Rajahs or Nawabs; the dues to the Church were certainly not less onerous than the tithes to the Brahmins. Nadir Shah's sack of Delhi—a foreign conqueror's revenge, by the way—was horrible; but not worse than the Constable de Bourbon's sack of Rome. Yet he would be a bold man who should urge that the Pax Romana, with its blight of the great slave-worked estates, and constant drain of wealth to the metropolis, was better for the mass of the people than even the turbulence and oppression of the period of the Crusades. Progress was going on all the time; and we can now see that what has often been called anarchy was but the commencement of a newer and more vigorous life, due to the barbarian invasion. It may be that our interference checked a similar development in India, following on the gradual break up of the Mogul Empire of Delhi. At any rate, we have no right to claim that we have benefited the country, until evidence has been given that the mass of the people are really better off under our domination than they were, or than they are, under native rule. That is the test of the merit of all governments, home or foreign. Do they or do they not secure increased welfare for the body of the people governed?

There is but one way in which to answer such a question, or to learn to appreciate our true relation to India; and that is by a careful study, without a tinge of national prejudice, of the real history of India and of our connection with the country. To do this effectively calls not only for industry but for imagination. It is difficult enough for us to comprehend another period of the history of our own race, here in our own country, to appreciate the different forms of production, to follow the varying relations of social life, to grasp the substance of the forms of government and administration at distant epochs. If this be so with our own people, how much harder is it to enter into the national life and development of a number of Asiatic nations bound together for a comparatively short time under our alien rule, but whose growth for thousands of years has gone on in conditions so entirely dissimilar, that it needs an effort of the mind to reach the period when the two civilisations had a common starting-point?

Our national characteristics are not favourable to such a comprehension as is really needed; and, great as has been the work done by some noble Englishmen in this field, it needs only to cite such a passage as follows to show the initial drawbacks which have to be surmounted in endeavouring to get to know the population. "Englishmen in India have less opportunity than might be expected of forming opinions of the native character. Even in England few know much of the people beyond their own class, and what they do know they learn from newspapers and publications of a description which does not exist in India. In that country, also, religion and manners put bars to our intimacy with the natives, and limit the number of transactions, as well as the free communication of opinions. We know nothing of the interior of families but by report, and have no share in those numerous occurrences of life in which the amiable parts of character are most exhibited. Missionaries of a different religion, judges, police magistrates, officers of revenue or customs, and even diplomatists, do not see the most virtuous portion of a native, nor any portion, unless when influenced by passion or occupied by some personal interest. What we do see we judge by our own standard. . . . It might be argued in opposition to many unfavourable testimonies that those who have known the Indians longest have always the best opinion of them ; but this is rather a compliment to human nature than to them, since it is true of every other people. It is more to the point, that all persons who have retired from India, think better of the people they have left after comparing them with others even of the most justly-admired nations." This was written by Mountstuart Elphinstone more than thirty years ago, but it is in the main as true now as it was then.

Again, in reference to mere taxation and administration, our difficulties of understanding, even after an experience of a hundred years, are surely very great, arising in part out of the very nature of the case. There is no more ardent admirer of the virtues—I had nearly added, and of the vices—of our rule in India than Sir Henry Maine. Yet he says that to him there is "the heaviest presumption against the existence in any part of India of a form of ownership conferring the exact rights on the proprietor which are given to the present English ownership in fee simple ;" and he shows the impossibility of arriving at any clear notion as to competitive rent in that country. Moreover, he gives the following admirable summary of the hopelessness of foreigners attempting to deal practically with that very land revenue which is the sheet-anchor of our revenue in India, as it has been of every Government that ruled the country before us. "Do you, on entering on the settlement of a new province, find that a peasant proprietary has been displaced by an oligarchy of vigorous usurpers, and do you think it expedient to take the Government dues from the once-oppressed yeomen ? The result is the immediate decline, and consequently bitter discontent of the class above them, who find themselves sinking to the level of mere annuitants on the land. Such was the land settlement of Oudh, which was shattered to pieces by the Sepoy mutiny of 1857, and which greatly affected its course. Do you, reversing this policy, arrange that the superior holder shall be answerable to Government? You find that you have created a landed aristocracy which has no parallel in wealth or power, except the proprietors of English soil. Of this nature is the more modern settlement of the province of Oudh only recently consummated, and such will ultimately be the position of the Talukdars or Barons, among whom its soil has been divided. Do you adopt a policy different from either of those which I have indicated, and make your arrangements with representatives of the village community? You find you have arrested a process of change which was steadily proceeding. You have given to this peculiar proprietary group a vitality which it was losing, and a stiffness to the relations of the various classes composing it which they never had before."*

In this brief historical sketch which is given as an introduction to a more exact examination of our present financial system in India, no pretence is made therefore to do more than summarise the main facts. Probably more than one generation will pass before it is possible to make a fair survey of our connection with the country and its results. When such a survey is made there is too much reason to

* Maine's "Village Communities," p. 150.

fear that the estimate of the value of our services to India will more nearly resemble that which we ourselves now place on the services rendered by the Spaniards to South America, than the exaggerated view of the beneficence of our administration which is generally taken among us to-day.

The first attempts of the English to establish direct trade with India were made in the reign of the Emperor Akbar. They were unsuccessful, nor was it until after the missions of Captain Hawkins and Sir Thomas Roe to the Court of Jehangir that a factory and settlement were obtained at Surat on favourable terms. Akbar's reign of fifty years was, in all probability, the most prosperous period for the mass of the people that had been seen since the downfall of the ancient Chalookya dynasty. This was chiefly due to the firmness with which he maintained his power, and to the justice and considerateness of his taxation. The settlement of the land revenue was carried out by the famous Rajah Ṭoder Mull, though there is little doubt that the arrangements were in existence before, and were only equitably reduced to order by him. According to the Code of Menu one-fifth of the produce could be taken; by Toder Mull's regulations one-third was nominally so taken on an average of ten years. This payment, which had gradually come to be made in money, was confirmed in that sense; though the proportion might be paid in kind if the money payment were alleged to be too onerous; and the exaction was very rarely pressed in hard times. Where the system of farming the revenue was the rule, both before and after these arrangements, a larger proportion was exacted, and in some exceptional cases the taxation was pushed to such a point that the villagers left their lands, and fled for the time, or until a better state of things was established.

Under Akbar's arrangement, with the addition of certain cesses on trades and other duties of the nature of an octroi, no less than £30,000,000 were paid annually into the Imperial treasury, nor, though the people were much more oppressed and the public peace was much more disturbed under his successors, is there any reason to believe that a less sum was collected by the various emperors of the Mogul dynasty until the great Mahratta conquests and the break up of the empire.* For one hundred and seventy years it is stated by competent authorities that this was the lowest amount of the Imperial revenue; and when the period is taken into consideration, as well as the large jaghires and rent-free grants given to favourites, this sum, drawn from 150,000,000 people at the outside, certainly represents a much larger revenue than has ever been collected under our rule.

Nevertheless, save immediately after some outbreak or invasion, there was no evidence that the country was impoverished; while during the whole period the manufactures of India were, as they had been for centuries before, sought after all over the

* Mr. W. W. Hunter, who is paid £3,000 a year as Director-General of the Statistical Department in Calcutta, partly in order that he may act as Advocate-General of the Indian Government in Edinburgh, puts Akbar's revenue at £42,000,000, and Aurungzib's revenue in all at £80,000,000 yearly, which of course strengthens the argument in the text.

earth. All the early travellers were struck by the display of wealth, and our rising industries were obliged to be protected against Indian competition. Aurungzib's renewal of the poll-tax on Hindoos, which had been abrogated by the wise tolerance of Akbar, was a most oppressive measure politically, and the system of farming the revenue again assumed dangerous and most harmful proportions towards the close of the dynasty; but it remains true that during the time that we were slowly working our way from being merchants to conquerors, India remained a wealthy country, with a revenue enormous in comparison with that of any European State, and with apparently a great power of rebound from any temporary misfortune, such as a Mahratta rising or an Afghan invasion. Nor should we overlook the fact, that in spite of much cruelty and rapine, the rivalry of the states and rajahs, the display of native courts, the magnificence of native architecture, gave a life and colour to the whole people such as is unknown in British India of our time.

This capacity of rapid recovery from disaster, which has been remarked before by all observers as a striking characteristic of India in the period prior to our invasion, was undoubtedly due to the permanence of the village community. The village community or township was the unit of early Aryan civilisation, as the *gens* was the unit of the social system in the Gentile organisation of savagery and barbarism. It formed, and in many districts still forms, a complete organism in itself, which can be grouped with, but never absorbed by, other similar organisms. The primitive communal arrangements on which they were based have been handed down from countless generations, and the manner in which the payment of land revenue to a chosen centre arose can now almost certainly be traced. In its origin the arrangement was democratic rather than monarchal. But what concerns us is the steady prosperity and marvellous continuity of these village communities, which were the main element of a society where the enormous majority of the population was agricultural. Thorough masters of their own method of tillage, and well able to deal with problems of irrigation in dry regions which our own engineers have so far failed to grapple with successfully, they are self-supporting, and practically independent of all outsiders. These little republics have each and all their headman, who is chiefly supported by the community which he represents in respect to the government, and administers in a popular way the business of the community in regard to the division of lands, the apportionment of water, etc. The accountant, the watchman, the priest, followed by the smith, the carpenter, the barber, the potter, and others, have all their places in the little society, who are all dependent for their support upon the agriculture of the group, and hand on their avocations from father to son from generation to generation.

If another village is formed, though the extent of territory and number of inhabitants may be different, the same functionaries are provided for, and all take their part in some way in the communal business. In such a case there is absolutely no complete property, but the whole village is responsible for the payment, through the headman, of its percentage of revenue on the crops calculated on land of three degrees of fertility. Clearly these village communities, when grouped in tens or hundreds under the old native system, might afford fine opportunities for plunder to a collector or zemindar of a pergunnah, as the group of a hundred was called. But, in spite of many instances of extortion, there is nothing to show that the country was exhausted by the demands made upon it, and the villages survived the raids and misgovernment of Afghan and Patan, Mogul, Sikh, and Mahratta, who might be masters and conquerors for a time, but the villages still lived on.

"In times of trouble they arm and fortify themselves; a hostile army passes through the country; the village communities collect their cattle within their walls, and let the enemy pass unprovoked. If plunder and devastation be directed against themselves, and the force employed be irresistible, they flee to friendly villages at a distance; but, when the storm has passed over, they return and resume their occupations. If a country remain for a series of years the scene of continued pillage and massacre, so that the villages cannot be inhabited, the scattered villagers nevertheless return whenever the power of peaceable possession revives. A generation may pass away, but the succeeding generation will return. The sons will take the places of their fathers; the same site for the village, the same position for the houses, the same lands will be reoccupied by the descendants of those who were driven out when the village was depopulated; and it is not a trifling matter that will drive them out, for they will often maintain their post through times of disturbance and convulsion, and acquire strength sufficient to resist pillage and oppression with success. This union of the village communities, each one forming a separate little state in itself, has, I conceive, contributed more than any other cause to the preservation of the people of India through all the revolutions and changes which they have suffered, and is in a high degree conducive to their happiness and to the enjoyment of a great portion of freedom and independence."*

Tyranny, lawlessness, and rapine might, in short, reign above, while below these conservative communes maintained almost unruffled the peaceful continuity of their existence. Nor should it be forgotten, that great as might be the temporary oppression exercised by the Government, the Rajah, the Nawab, or the Zemindar, the agricultural wealth extorted from the villagers was at least used in the country, and expended on retainers and others. Bad in every way as many of the Mahommedan rulers of India were prior to the Mogul dynasty, they at least lived in the country, and Nadir Shah's loot of Delhi was quite an exceptional event, as well it might be.

Consequently we find that during the whole period from the first English acquaintance with India through the reigns of Jehangir, Shah Jehan, Aurungzib, and Mohammed Shah, until in the last century we began to compete with the French for the supremacy, the records of impoverishment and famine are but trifling. Here again the popular opinion is, to a great extent, incorrect. Aurungzib was a powerful but harsh and bad ruler; he imposed obnoxious taxes, and ravaged with cruelty the terri-

* Sir Charles Metcalfe.

tories of those who had revolted against him; the Mahratta cavalry were no respecters of persons, and their tribute or chout was levied upon all with complete indifference to anybody's welfare but their own; the weakness of the central power, when the Moguls were tottering to their fall, gave functionaries in Hyderabad, in Bengal, and other territories, opportunity to rob and fleece the inhabitants; and at a later date the Mahommedan adventurers of Seringapatam acted as seemed good in their own eyes until they came into collision with the English power. But through all this long period of tumult and intestine war, of good government under Akbar, and of apparent anarchy during the Mahratta raids, the records of really serious dearth or famine are few and far between. Prior to the present century famine was rare in India.

Not only did the village communities and the Government provide in numberless cases against periods of drought and flood by storage of grain, but even the harshest native ruler, for his own sake, and almost as a matter of course, lessened, or even failed to make, his demand when even trifling scarcity threatened. Much as the method of collection might vary, this judicious laxity may be said to have been almost invariably practised in Native States, as it is now. When the oppression was carried beyond bounds insurrection against the local tyrant was still possible, and not unfrequently successful.

From the Himalayas to Cape Comorin, and from the slopes of Assam to the Persian Gulf, the agricultural population, with their simple but beautiful arts, growing up naturally out of their society, were generally in a prosperous condition. In the great towns

Benares, Delhi, Agra, etc., were to be seen wealth, luxury, and public display scarcely to be equalled even at the end of the seventeenth century in Paris, London, or Vienna. The state of the communications was bad, no doubt; and as the country became more disturbed after the great Mahratta risings and the increasing imbecility of the Mogul rulers, the great tanks and irrigation works in many districts were beginning to fall into decay; but India had passed through many worse crises, and would certainly have risen above this.

With the eighteenth century began the great rivalry between England and France in the East, which practically involved the question as to which should have the mastery of India. At first glance the odds seemed greatly against the English, for our command of the sea was not then by any means so complete as it afterwards became, and the French had unquestionably greater power in the Native Courts than the English. But our men were backed up more from home, they showed in emergencies extraordinary capacity; and thus was seen the marvellous spectacle of clerks and supercargoes developing into generals and administrators of the first rank, and winning an empire against fearful odds. This unexampled fashion of conducting the business of a trading company, taking possession of an empire as a detail of business, and waging great wars to secure dividends for shareholders, cannot here be adequately dealt with. Nothing like it had ever before been seen in the East. It was a fitting continuation, in many of its phases, of the earlier conquests of the commercial classes of Europe.

For from the first began that steady withdrawal of wealth from India to England which in one shape or another has gone on ever since. Throughout the latter part of the eighteenth century, the wealthy nabob, who had returned to this country after shaking the pagoda-tree to some purpose, was the familiar type of the rich man of yesterday. And there are the records of the East India Company, open to all the world, to bear witness as to the conduct of the fortune-hunters of that halcyon period. India was the El Dorado of the unscrupulous commercial adventurer. The "legitimate" proceedings of the company chartered by Queen Elizabeth and continued to our own time were bad enough, as the most strenuous supporters of that famous body must be forced to admit. It was no rose-water management which paid such enormous dividends, and drove the stock of the shareholders to an unheard-of premium. But the illegitimate business was infinitely worse until checked by stern action on the part of the Government and the directors. Even the lowest commercial morality cannot justify the direct robbery and rascality which pervaded every department of our administration from the time of Clive's rise to power until the first governor-generalship of Lord Cornwallis.

It is unnecessary to debate whether Warren Hastings could or could not have avoided the transactions stigmatised by Burke; holding the position which they did, it is useless to discuss whether Clive and smaller men were entitled to be "amazed at their own moderation." The guilt or innocence of individuals counts for little in such a wholesale system of plunder in gross and in detail as afflicted the provinces under our immediate control, and particularly Bengal and Oude, between 1757 and 1786. What the total amount of wealth may have been which was transported from India to England in one form or another during the latter half of the last century will never be known; but that it was something unparalleled since the great discoveries of the sixteenth century there is abundant evidence to show.

And here, before touching upon the growth of our domination and the administrative changes by which it was accompanied, it is well to recall the fact that the English conquered India with the Indian troops and with the aid of native alliances. Our Sepoy army, admirably drilled and led, did wonders, and turned defeat into victory on many a hard-fought field. The Europeans were, to use Kinglake's expression, the head of the lance; but they would have been quite useless without the handle afforded by the native troops. Of their courage, devotion, and self-sacrifice all our generals have spoken in the highest terms. At Plassey and Assaye, at Wandiwash and Seringapatam, as in the Punjab and during the astounding campaigns in Nepaul, our native troops have shown themselves well worthy to march side by side with the flower of the English army; and more than once, as at the siege of Bhurtpore, have advanced to victory when the Englishmen themselves had fallen back. The silly notion that we could have conquered or held the country, but for the courage and loyalty of the native troops and camp-followers, is a delusion of recent growth, and one which, it is safe to say, has never been shared by a military man who had any knowledge of the facts.

Whatever his defects, and they were many and great, Warren Hastings was the first Englishman who seems to have fully appreciated what we were doing in India, and who set to work in a serious and statesmanlike spirit to turn our happy-go-lucky system of commercial intrigue and trade chicanery, backed up by an army of mercenaries, into an administration worthy of a nascent empire. If he bullied and robbed the rich and powerful, he at least endeavoured to relieve the mass of the agriculturists under his control from the infinite mischiefs arising out of the combination of English and native misrule. His attempts were, as unfortunately nearly all our attempts have been, far too much imbued with the harmful spirit of Europeanisation. But it is at least remarkable, that from that day to this his name has been reverenced throughout India as that of a great man who was just to the people. The truth was, that, hampered by instructions from home, and constantly at his wits' end for money to meet the many combinations formed against him, he could not carry out his own views even partially. It was left, therefore, for Lord Cornwallis to reduce the system of government to more complete order, and to lay the foundation of that well-paid and arrogant, but, on the whole, pecuniarily honest bureaucracy which has administered our ever-growing empire in the East for the last hundred years. Landing in India in 1786, he at once set to work to reform the abuses which still remained unchecked. A liberal scale of salaries for Europeans took the place of the previous system of licensed plunder. After the successful war against Tippoo, in which, by the way, we had the assistance of the Mahrattas and the Nizam, Lord Cornwallis continued his reorganisation of the administration in Bengal and other districts, many of the judicial arrangements being great improvements on the previous system of Sir Elijah Impey.

But Lord Cornwallis' main administrative achievement will always be considered the Permanent Land Settlement in Bengal. This much-debated measure has been looked upon from very different points of view since its first enactment in 1793. It was, in fact, a huge blunder. The revenue collectors with whom he made the permanent settlement, thus turning them into owners of the soil and constituting them a landed aristocracy, were in reality not more owners of the soil than the peasants whom they represented, and from whom they collected the revenue; nor was their position secure save during good behaviour. They could be, and were, removed if they failed to satisfy the Government or the villagers. The infrequency of such removals was no evidence of the permanence of their position, still less, assuredly, of their claim to be dealt with as sole owners of the soil at a fixed payment for ever, with the right to treat all below them as mere tenants subject to their will. Yet this was the position which, in spite of all protests, the Board of Directors authorised Lord Cornwallis to give the zemindars. The result has been that we not only created a landed aristocracy of the most oppressive kind where none of a similar character had existed before, placing the ryots at the mercy of these men so long as the light Government tax was paid, but we shut ourselves out from taking advantage of any improvement that might be made in this rich province. So that for nearly one hundred years the revenue of Bengal has remained stationary, while the descendants of the zemindars have become great landowners, determined, as we have lately seen, to oppose to the last any intervention on the part of the Government to protect their tenants. Of the "aristocracy" thus created at the expense of the serious impoverishment of the ryots the less said the better. With few exceptions they are a worthless set.*

But the permanent settlement has protected the province from excessive taxation, though the advantage of this has been derived precisely by those who ought not to have been benefited. Had the arrangement been made with the zemindars, simply as representatives of the districts, they being allowed a percentage for collection, with no power to raise rents without the consent of the Government, then no doubt a permanent settlement would have greatly benefited the whole people. As it was, this was our first great fiscal blunder in India, so far as the interests of the agricultural population of Bengal were concerned; and it arose, as so many of our

* A province like Bengal proper, where the village system has fallen to pieces of itself, was the proper field for the creation of a peasant proprietary; but Lord Cornwallis turned it into a country of great estates, and was compelled to take his landlords from the tax-gatherers of his worthless predecessors. (Sir H. Maine, "Village Communities," p. 154.)

blunders in India have arisen, from a stern determination to regard all its social, economical, and political problems from a European point of view. A similar remark would apply to the judicial arrangements, especially, as will be seen later, those which deal with the enforcement of contracts and the collection of debts.

In Madras an exactly opposite course was taken with reference to the people to be settled with, and the arrangement for payment of land taxation was made with the ryots themselves. The amount demanded was, in the first instance, equal to a third of the crop, and the settlement occasioned intolerable oppression. In fact, Sir Thomas Munro's first measures read like the edicts of the Egyptians against the Jews. One-third of the crop was excessive for a permanent demand by itself; but in addition to this the ryot was taxed on the land sown, not in accordance with the value of the land. Further, all sorts of restrictions and compulsory penal regulations as to cultivation were imposed that were nothing short of ruinous to the people. It is true that these most obnoxious regulations were changed within five years. But five years of such blundering was enough to shake all confidence, and to reduce a large part of the population to misery. Moreover, even when the change was made many objectionable features were left untouched, and the year-to-year settlement, which is a hopeless form of tenure in India unless made with the lightest hand, was maintained. Thus, to quote a writer whose knowledge of and sympathy with the people of India have perhaps never been exceeded by any

Englishman, "The ancient hereditary rights and practices fell into desuetude; while it is certain that the new system not only perpetuated the evils of the immediately preceding exactive native governments, but actually exceeded them. There were gross errors in regard to the land settlements in Bengal and in the North-West Provinces; but it is questionable whether anything so universally depressing and demoralising as the ryotwary system of Madras was ever attempted there." To its demoralising and depressing effects the province of Madras still bears testimony, as there is but too much reason to know.

Better arrangements were made in Bombay and other parts of India, the assessments being levied with more regard to the interests of the people, though still for short terms, and with insufficient attention to remission in bad seasons. But why were they better? Just because they reverted in some degree to the more equitable native methods, encouraged instead of thwarting cultivation, and left the ryots more to their own devices, the Government being content to take a fair revenue from the chief landholders without excessive interference with the habits of the agriculturists. The ravages of war during the period now being treated of—between 1793 and 1830—had made care and consideration in this respect more essential than ever.

And here I may briefly deal with a gross economical error which, to their shame be it said, still finds its way into the most important reports of the very highest officials. It is argued that the land revenue of India is not a tax at all, but that it is merely "rent," and therefore cannot be reckoned as any real imposition on the people. The Government or the State is the landlord, and in taking the land tax it exacts only what the landlord would take if the State did not! It is difficult to deal seriously with such nonsense as this. As usual it arises from our determination to apply English views and English theories to a totally different economical and social system. In England land is rented for the purpose of making a profit on the market, just as a factory or a workshop might be rented; and the landlord takes a certain proportion of the profit made by the capitalist, in this case a farmer, in return for the use of the profit-making machine of which he has private possession. And the landlord and the farmer get, the one his rent, the other his profit on his capital out of the ill-paid labour of the agricultural hind, who forms the third member in this trinity of production for profit on the land.

This is still quite an exceptional form of dealing with the land in all countries but England; and the theory of rent, which is usually identified with the name of Ricardo, besides being of far inferior value and correctness to that which some imagine, is even, with the fullest admission, partially applicable only in a country such as ours, where the capitalist system has been developed to the highest degree. Even so, let us suppose that the Government calls upon the landlord to pay a large or a small proportion of his rent for the purposes of administration, is not that a tax? Clearly it is. If, refusing to treat the landlord as a separate individual, and dealing with the three persons engaged in cultivation as one whole, the State says—one-fifth of the gross crop will be taken for purposes of administration to be paid in money, the average being struck over a period of so many years, settle it between you how the proportion is to be divided,—would not that be a tax? Just as clearly. Well then, in India, where the ryots, as a rule, grow their crops to supply their family or to exchange merely for such simple articles as they require, the State says such and such a fraction is needed for administration, pay it over to the revenue collector—is not that a tax? The matter is too clear for dispute.

The ryot, who in a bad year—or now, alas! often in a good year—has to go short of food or salt to pay the Government demand, knows very well that it is a tax that he is paying. And not being, like the capitalist farmer, a man of means, who can shift off elsewhere when he finds his rent too onerous, it is a matter of perfect indifference to him whether the amount which is taken from him to keep up an enormous European army, or to remit to pensioners or shareholders in England, is called "rent" or "tax." It is enough for him to know that he is left with an empty belly because the State takes too large a share of his scanty produce to itself. Whether under a native or under a British Government, a land tax is a land tax, and no amount of foolish trickery with economical terminology, can alter that fact.

The main point of interest, however, to the natives during the period from 1757 was that an ever-increasing portion of India fell under the English tax-gatherer. The land revenue, the salt monopoly, the minor duties—all came under our control. The records of conquest, brilliant as they may be, are but the exciting introduction to the plain work of administration. None will deny that such men as Lord Wellesley, Lord Hastings, and above all Lord William Bentinck, were inspired with a sincere desire to benefit the people under their rule; while it is equally certain that neither the heads of the Great Company Bahadur at home nor the English Government were anxious for that persistent extension of territory which has hitherto seemed inevitable. Nor do the natives of India themselves dispute that in many respects the rule of the East India Company over the territories acquired from Mahommedan, Sikh, and Mahratta has been better than that of the Mogul Emperors or the successful Hindoo or Mahommedan adventurers who followed them. But we must not overlook the facts, that as the English domination advanced, the natives were, as a rule, shut out from the more important civil offices; that the career of arms was also closed to them so far as concerned the higher grades of the service; that a new and, to the natives, a revolting system of jurisprudence was introduced; and that, above all, rebellion against oppression became hopeless.

All Lord William Bentinck's noble reforms, returning in many particulars to the happy period of Akbar, could not change these facts to any appreciable extent, nor could the truth that foreigners were in possession of the country, who would never be thoroughly at home there, be disguised. Furthermore, during the first half of this century an economical competition was going on which was crueller in its effects than any foreign invasion which had ever afflicted the dwellers in Hindostan.

In the seventeenth, and during a great part of the eighteenth century, the importation of Indian calicoes into England was actually prohibited on the distinct ground that their competition would have crushed our rising industry in similar goods. At the end of the eighteenth century, however, England had become possessed of a monopoly of new machinery, which enabled her to undersell the whole world in goods of nearly every description. Our own hand-loom weavers and spinners suffered terribly from the competition of these machines at their own door. But their miseries were child's play in comparison with the horrors inflicted on the weavers of India by our unchecked competition with the native goods at a little later date. The poor creatures saw their means of livelihood taken from them by a process which they themselves never understood. Tens of thousands of them perished; for there was no place for them in the Indian society of that day apart from that which they occupied. There was no attempt made by the Government to regulate this competition, and the effects of the English connection in this regard have been wholly harmful to the people—monstrous as such a statement may seem to the free-trader, whose highest ideal of happiness for the human race is that all should make profits by cheating their neighbours. But the frightful results of mere indifference to the action of economical causes are, as a rule, overlooked. The terrible Afghan War, with its long legacy of debt and disaffection, the conquest of the

Punjab and the annexation of Scinde—such matters quite eclipse the sad fate of the unfortunate Indian weavers, who perished silently on the battlefield of commercial war.

It is the same with famines and the other evils brought about under our management. They are looked upon as due to "natural laws," over which human beings have no control whatever. We attribute all suffering under native governments to native mis-rule; our own errors we father on "Nature." Thus there probably never was known a worse period of native rule than that which afflicted Oude for forty years prior to our annexation in 1856. Robbery, torture, fiendish barbarities of every kind were inflicted upon the wretched inhabitants. The horrors recorded by Sir William Sleeman would be taken nowadays, as they were then, to justify our interposition ten times over. But the land tax was roughly, and, in the native sense, not unreasonably taken after all, the rapacity of money-lenders was held in check, the laws were understood. "There were neither accumulating arrears of land revenue nor ruinous back debts, to weigh down the proprietors; there were no unsatisfied decrees of court to drive debtors to hopeless despair; they came back from their court of bankruptcy, the jungle forest, free from encumbrances; the bread tax was fixed with some regard to the coming harvest; arrears were remitted when the impossibility of payment within the year was clearly demonstrated." Further, "there could be no black despair in those days of changeful misrule." What, then, do we find? Why, that, in spite of all the oppression and unspeakable atrocities, Sir William Sleeman records that "the people generally, or at least a great part of them, would prefer to reside in Oudh, under all the risks to which these contests expose them, than in our own districts, under the evils the people are exposed to from the uncertainties of our law, the multiplicity and formality of our courts, the pride and negligence of those who preside over them, and the corruption and insolence of those who must be employed to prosecute or defend a cause in them, and to enforce the fulfilment of a decree when passed." Once more he says, "I am persuaded that if it were put to the vote among the people of Oudh, ninety-nine in a hundred would rather remain as they are, without any feeling of security in life or property, than have our system introduced in its present complicated state."

All this is forgotten at the present time, and the pernicious Anglo-Indian cabal exercises its great influence in the press to stifle any revival of the truth. But the fact that when the complicated system was introduced the agricultural population of Oudh declared against us, is conclusive evidence of the truth of Sir William Sleeman's appreciation of the situation in that great province. Though during the Mutiny the agriculturists over the greater part of India were certainly not hostile, it is, I believe, impossible to point to a single instance in which annexation was welcomed by the people; but there are many in which the direct rule of a European without the introduction of European methods was accepted with rejoicing, and would gladly have been maintained.

This the ablest of the old East India Company's servants, many of whom were men who knew, loved, and were implicitly trusted by the people of India, saw clearly. More than this, their views found favour with the Board of Directors at home. Despatch after despatch from home, remonstrance after remonstrance on the spot, might be given, showing that great as were the reforms that had been made in our methods in some respects since the earlier periods, the men who were mostly deeply versed in Indian administration, such as the great Sir Henry Lawrence (to name a name revered by men of all schools), were opposed to taking the complete control of new districts, and to filling the highest posts with well-paid European officials. But the annexation party had a tight grip of the administrative machine, and never failed to make use of it to extend our direct domination whenever and wherever they could. This was the case even prior to the advent of Lord Dalhousie as Governor-General; but with his accession to power the policy took a range and scope unknown before.

Hitherto our annexations had followed war and conquest, or had been due to deed of gift from the supreme power. Now it followed hard upon intrigue and chicane, or the enforcement of the doctrine of "lapse," when a native ruler had no heir, and was not permitted to adopt any. Lord Dalhousie was a man of bitter temper and boundless ambition, utterly incapable of looking at India from other than a bureaucrat's point of view. It was the mission, therefore, of this arbitrary bigot to overthrow all the best traditions of our rule in India, to shock every native idea of justice or good faith, to commence that course of unscrupulous annexation and wholesale Europeanisation from which our empire is now suffering, and to lead up by his policy to one of the most serious rebellions that ever shook the power of any Government. For with Lord Dalhousie began in earnest that "development" of India by railways, barracks, irrigation works, and the like, which have undoubtedly rendered our hold upon the country more secure, and give certain advantages to the people, but which have heaped debt upon the Exchequer, have led to the employment of an excessive number of our countrymen, and have largely increased that drain of produce to England, which is the most dangerous and deplorable feature of our connection with India.

At the time nothing was seen of the drawbacks to all this. Oudh, the Berars, Scinde, Nagpur, Satara, Jhansi, were all taken on one pretext or another, the railway system was begun on a most expensive plan, and when Lord Dalhousie took his departure from the empire which he had done his best to ruin, he issued a proclamation in laudation of his own exploits as an administrator, worthy to be ranked for magniloquence with the windy declamation of Elijah Pogram. India, in his eyes, was a fitting subject for experiment, and a great country with three thousand years of history behind it was placed at the absolute disposal of a second-rate War Office clerk.

Scarcely had Lord Dalhousie turned his back upon Calcutta when the great mutiny of the Sepoy army broke out. It was a rising against which the

English Government had been warned, but it took the official classes quite by surprise. Put down as it was with marvellous vigour but relentless severity, it could not have been suppressed at all had other provinces shown the spirit of Oudh, or had the men of India displayed the courage and initiative of the Ranee of Jhansi. Certainly a great opportunity for insurrection was offered, and it must be admitted that the rule of the East India Company, in spite of many drawbacks, could not have been intolerable, or, notwithstanding the prestige of former success, local risings of the natives would frequently have taken place during the doubtful period of the siege of Delhi and the advance to the relief of Lucknow. The ryots grumbled at the mistakes made, and recognised—this was a universal complaint—that the periods of prosperity known in old days had somehow disappeared; but they were not driven from their homes, they had not yet suffered such infamous extortion as led to Wasadeo Bulwunt's rising ten years ago, and—which is a permanent reason for quietude—the natives of India are in the habit of submitting to grievous oppression before taking action on their own behalf. The result we all know. English domination was more solidly established than ever, and the rule of Company merged in the supremacy of the Crown.

In the hundred years between Plassy and the Mutiny much had been learnt by the abler men at home who were responsible for the conduct of Indian affairs. They had learnt, for one thing, that India under their rule, not enjoying the great advance in mechanical appliances which was changing the whole face of production in Europe, had become a very poor country. Economy in every direction was a canon of their policy, and it is safe to say, that had the views of the Board and its ablest advisers prevailed, adventurous Governor-Generals would have been kept in check. Not a few, too, had come to understand, like Elphinstone, that our hold upon India could not be permanent, and that the noblest career we could possibly hope for Englishmen as a body, or for England as a nation, was to prepare the way to a reconstitution of the native governments under English guidance. When, therefore, the Crown took over the control of India, John Stuart Mill wrote what was in effect a defence of the old East India Company, whose servant he had been. That document is well worthy of attention at the present time, for many of the warnings it contains have been justified by events, and the experience of such a man and of those who stood behind him was at least worthy of consideration then.

The East India Company had been, in the main, an economical administrator, and the drain of produce from India to England during the generation prior to its downfall was trifling compared to what it was at the end of the last century, or to what it has been since 1858. Parliamentary misgovernment and capitalist loans at home, despotic bureaucracy and wholesale Europeanisation in India, have been more harmful by far than all the strange anomalies of the Company's Raj. Indeed, mischievous as I hold our annexation policy to have been alike to India and to England, deeply as I deplore the blunders made in the land settlements and in our civil and criminal courts, it is impossible to study the administration of India from 1826 to 1857, and to read the noble careers of the many great men who were proud to serve it, without being able to appreciate in some degree that loyalty and enthusiasm for the old East India Company which still stirs those, alike natives and Europeans, who stood by the Company in the trying days of the great Mutiny. Its faults were those of the time and of the commercial polity; its merits were a credit to our nation and mankind.

The system of administration bequeathed by the Company to the Crown in India, was virtually that which had been established by Lord Cornwallis in 1796. During those sixty years, as our territory extended, the same methods of military organisation and civil government were applied to the new districts, with but slight modifications of detail. His reforms have been merely noted in passing, but how necessary they were may be judged from the statement of Colonel Chesney, one of the most earnest defenders of English rule in India: "The earlier members of the Indian service, civil and military, must be pronounced to have been the most corrupt body of officials that ever brought disgrace upon a civilised government."

Lord Cornwallis changed all this, and after the Mahratta War, nine years later, "the duties of territorial government took the place of buying and selling as the leading pursuit of the Company's servants." This was in 1805. The Empire of India now consists of ten great provinces, each of which has its own civil government. There are still the three "Presidencies," with the Viceroy or Governor-General in Council at Calcutta. Simla, the Governor of Bombay, and the Governor of Madras, and the three Presidency armies, are still maintained. But the civil administration is carried on by the Governors of Bombay and Madras, the Lieutenant-Governors, and the Chief Commissioners. Under them there are 870 covenanted Indian civilians, so called because they enter into a covenant before going to India,—first entered upon by Clive in 1765,—and form the direct official descendants of the first regular thirty of the old East India Company. They serve in the regulation provinces, and are now taken by competitive examination instead of by appointment, as formerly. But outside these nine hundred covenanted civil servants there are many thousands of uncovenanted civilians in the provincial service, whose position is, in some respects, anomalous, though they hold places of the greatest importance and responsibility, and their official status is not yet recognised. India is, in fact, under the control, in spite of all reforms, of a multitude of Europeans, who themselves hold no thoroughly assured position theoretically, though in practice powerful enough. It is the district officers and judges, the collectors and police officials, the administrators of public works and the managers of the railways, who are the real rulers of India. They form an enormous foreign bureaucracy, worked with great skill as a machine, but with even more than the usual defects incident to a bureaucracy. Some account of their duties, and the manner in which they perform them, will be found in the following pages.

Looking back over the history of our connection with the country, with the renewals at intervals of the Company's Charter, we cannot fail to be struck with the apparently unconscious character of our action. Here and there, an able man, such as Sleeman or Geddes, has understood that the destruction of native rule was by no means an unmixed benefit; the administrators at home have constantly protested against the proceedings of a Wellesley or a Dalhousie; but still the pressure of circumstances has pushed us relentlessly on, until our frontiers are practically conterminous with the great Russian Empire on one side, and the great Chinese Empire on the other. Never, even in the days of the most complete Mahommedan ascendancy, was the rule of one power recognised so completely from one end of the great peninsula to the other. But never, also, was the responsibility of this domination less felt by those upon whose shoulders it rests, and who will have to bear the brunt of any great catastrophe which may come to arouse their indifference.

I.

THE CONDITION OF INDIA.

SINCE 1874 the Bengal famine, the visit of the Prince of Wales, the proclamation of the Queen as Empress at Delhi, the frightful dearth, far exceeding both in extent and intensity that of Bengal, which for more than two years afflicted Madras and Bombay, the ordering of the Indian contingent to Malta, and other more recent events have had the effect of keeping India before the minds of the English people. The movement of the Indian troops at the crisis of the Eastern difficulty, served to manifest more clearly than anything else the intimate connection which now subsists between ourselves and our greatest dependency.

Lord Beaconsfield, by calling in Asia to redress the balance of military power in Europe, threw into the strongest relief the direct responsibility which rests upon Englishmen of all classes for treating India as an integral portion of the empire. That great and populous country depends absolutely upon us for good government, moderate taxation, and consideration of its general needs. Any blunders which we make affect 190,000,000 fellow-subjects, and are wholly irremediable save by ourselves.

Insurrection against unintentional oppression or well-meant injustice is hopeless, and the natives have no appeal but to the capacity and openness of mind of us, their conquerors, to remove any grievances from which they may be suffering. It is essential for them that, in spite of other topics, the serious consideration of the relation which England bears to India and the future policy which ought to be pursued, should be forced upon the nation.

India in 1878 had been for fully twenty years under the direct administration of the Queen and Parliament. In 1858 the famous proclamation was issued which finally transferred the supreme authority from the old East India Company to the Crown, its only possible substitute. The twenty years between those two dates were, so far as the internal condition of India is concerned, a period of more than Roman peace. The few frontier expeditions rendered necessary by the turbulence of wild tribes beyond our border were little more than reminders that all Asia does not belong to us. All that could be gained by profound peace ought therefore to have been already secured. Between 1858 and 1878 we constructed nearly 7,000 miles of railway through the country, connecting all the great cities and provinces; we carried out vast irrigation works intended to act as a general preventive of the dangerous effects of drought; and we laid down besides a whole network of ordinary agricultural roads. No effort, indeed, has been spared to develop our great dependency according to the most approved modern methods; and none can doubt that, although too frequently a bad inclination has been shown at home to charge India with expenses which do not rightly fall upon her, there has been a most earnest desire on the part of our officials in that country to raise the condition of the great body of the people, and thus to make them thoroughly contented with our rule. It has been universally felt that we must depend for the stability of our government on the good-will of the people even more than on our own strength.

We are constantly assured that we have succeeded in this noble attempt; that the natives of India are not only peaceful, but prosperous under the control of England; that in particular the cultivators are, as a class, far richer than they were; that the traders are at least equally flourishing; and that, generally, the great population of Hindostan, notwithstanding the necessarily increased taxation, due to a superior and more highly organised administration, is in every respect better off than when Lord Canning took up the reins of government.

All this Englishmen, as a rule, believe, and some of the benefits which we have conferred upon India are so obvious that the rest might not unfairly be taken for granted. Knowing that no harm is meant, it seems impossible that the gravest harm should be done.

But of late more detailed interest is taken in the subject, and it has been noted that almost every Indian official who has left the service and is free from the cares of administration openly gives it as his opinion that taxation in some directions has reached its utmost limit, even if it be not already too heavy for the simplest well-being of the agricultural classes; that although there is no evidence to show that the seasons from 1858 to 1878 were exceptional, the famines in almost every part of India were unprecedented in number and probably unequalled in severity; that, so far as can be judged, the supply of cattle for agricultural purposes has dwindled considerably as well as gone off in quality; that in many districts the ordinary scale of nourishment is below what it was some years ago, approaching dangerously near the limit of permanent starvation; and that there are not wanting grave indications as to the deterioration of the soil all over India, owing to excessive cropping, want of fallows, and insufficiency of manure. These and other equally serious symptoms have occasioned the gravest uneasiness to those who have observed them.

Even Lord Northbrook, certainly far from an economical viceroy, who said, in 1877, with all the authority derived from his high position and wide experience, that he "did not think any one who had any knowledge of the subject could doubt that the expenditure on the Indian railways was one of the most profitable investments that ever was made by a great nation," and further asserted that "in his opinion the finances of India were in a perfectly sound condition"—even Lord Northbrook was compelled by the urgency of the case to protest against our financial policy as involving the gravest danger, and to move a resolution to that effect in the House of Lords. Twelve months could not so entirely change the situation in such a matter. The previous circumstances must have been very critical indeed. They both were and are most critical.

For where is the wealth of India? The cultivators clearly have not got it, for they, as is generally admitted, can scarcely support the pressure of the present taxation, and over large tracts are so miserably destitute that they come upon the Government relief works at the very commencement of the slightest scarcity. There are no beautiful tombs or temples to point to, as in former ages, on which the savings of the population might have been lavished, nor are public works of general utility now built to any extent by private individuals. Indian investments are almost unknown. Barely a fraction of the enormous debt is held by natives; the capital for the railroads and irrigation works has all been borrowed in England; such cotton mills or other machinery as have hitherto been put up in our territory are, for the most part, dependent on the same source of supply; and the native manufactures, which have been ruined by our cheaper goods, are not yet, at any rate, replaced by new industries. Indian capital, if it is accumulating, acts very differently from capital elsewhere, seeing that it certainly does not compete to any extent for the most remunerative employment, and thus lower the interest on loans in the great industry of the country—tillage of the soil.

The main features of this state of things were well put some years ago in an article in the *Quarterly Review*:—"The wealth of native bankers and capitalists is on paper only—in brief, it is lent to their more needy countrymen. It represents the capital required for the agriculture of the millions of small farmers. If we trace downwards and downwards the wealth of the millionaire banker, we shall find it at last in thousands of miserable bullocks and such-like investments, the working stock of a numerous but very poor people."

And even this supply of capital, used at rates varying from 12 to 60 per cent., so far from increasing is getting smaller, though maybe the remainder is concentred in fewer hands. What effect these rates of interest, in conjunction with our rigid system of law, produce upon the cultivators, has been shown by Miss Florence Nightingale and other writers. But the causes of all the misery which they have enlarged upon lie far deeper than the village usurer.

The truth is that Indian society, as a whole, has been frightfully impoverished under our rule, and that the process is going on now at an increasingly rapid rate.

The natives say, and have said for years, that, as a whole, life has become harder since the English took the country. They are right; it has become harder, and will become harder still if we proceed on our present lines. They say also that the taxation is already crushing. That is true, too, and it has become yet more crushing in this present year. We, a business people, are forcing the cultivators to borrow at 12, 24, 60 per cent. of their native money-lenders, to build and pay the interest on the cost of vast public works which have never paid nearly 5 per cent.; we overlook entirely the tremendous economical drain which has been going on for a century owing to a foreign rule, and we neglect to consider that, as land gets poorer, the assessment rises in proportion to the produce. The dangers we have to face are grave indeed; no exaggeration, no forced rhetoric, is needed to increase the weight with which they must press upon us all. There is evidence enough already and to spare, whilst we are staggering on with our committees and commissions to a catastrophe which, unless facts and figures utterly lie, will be unequalled in the history of the world.

When poverty-smitten cultivators in one part of India are taxed—permanently taxed—to support famine-stricken ryots in another, who in their turn are to be taxed again for the like service, the whole country being drained all the while by enormous military charges, home charges, interest, remittances, and loss by exchange, it needs no great economist, no far-seeing statesman, to predict that a crash is inevitable. The famines which have been devastating India are in the main financial famines. Men and women cannot get food because they have not been able to save the money to buy it. Yet we are driven, so we say, to tax these people more. The great Irish famine of 1847 was often predicted, and none gave heed. The facts relating to India lie open to all men. It is not yet perhaps too late to deal with them, but there is assuredly no time to be lost.

At the very threshold of an inquiry into the condition of India, the almost insuperable difficulty is encountered, that there are scarcely any early official statistics with relation to population and produce. Though we have been the leading power in India for upwards of a hundred years, it is impossible to state with confidence whether the population is increasing, decreasing, or stationary.* This by itself is a most serious matter. There is a very general and probably well-founded impression that, owing to the long-continued peace, with early marriages and no infanticide, the people have largely increased in numbers under our rule; but there is positively no direct evidence whatever to this effect, and many careful observers altogether dispute the assumption. The only trustworthy figures are those of the general census of 1871, and these of course afford no criterion either way. In any case, the position will not be greatly affected if the population is taken as stationary for the whole twenty years 1858-78, at the amount of that census—namely, 190,000,000.

But the next point is in greater confusion still. The facts in relation to agricultural and other produce have never been tabulated with any approach to accuracy. The Statistical Abstract relating to British India, though fairly complete in other respects, gives absolutely nothing under this head, and the statistical departments here and in India seem quite unable to supplement the deficiency, though ready and even anxious to give every information. The almost incalculable importance of this omission will appear in the following pages, but the lack of such official data in the returns of a government which derives nearly one-half of its net revenue from the rent or taxation of the soil is surely not very creditable to us. In default of these, it becomes necessary to use such outside calculations as

* This has been remedied by the census of 1881.

have been made from time to time. Now these calculations, worked out at various times by independent authorities, rate the value of the total average gross produce of India during recent years at £300,000,000. Mr. Grant Duff, who cannot be accused of having ever erred in taking a too gloomy view of Indian finance, adopted these figures in 1871, as presenting a favourable view of the case. They have been accepted as not widely differing from an accurate estimate by the authorities at Calcutta; and generally they may be relied upon as giving a safe, though if anything rather sanguine, estimate of the average gross value of Indian produce, agricultural and manufactured, during the ten years.

It is not a little remarkable that a singularly able native writer,* who has been at the pains to work through all the attainable statistics of production, official and other, has arrived at almost identically the same conclusion by two different routes. He, too, gives this gross sum of £300,000,000 as a favourable average. The calculations as to the amount and value of produce made by him, though necessarily rough in some respects owing to insufficient data, are so far superior to anything to be found elsewhere, that the results arrived at with reference to the year 1867-68—a *good season* year, better indeed than any which we have had since—are valuable. The figures are in every instance put in excess of what might be taken as a good result on irrigated and unirrigated land. The following table shows the amount of acreage and return for all India.

* Mr. Dadabhai Naoroji.

	Acreage under cultivation.	Value of Produce.
Central Provinces . . .	12,378,215	16,000,000
Punjab	20,957,735	36,000,000
North-west Provinces . .	24,177,161	40,000,000
Bengal . . . . say	56,000,000	96,00 0000
Madras . . . say	18,000,000	36,000,000
Bombay	19,114,113	40,000,000
Oudh	7,991,040	13,000,000
Total	158,618,264	£277,000,000

Here is an entire agricultural produce of £277,000,000 for 158,618,264 acres, or at the rate of £1 14*s.* an acre. This seems an absurdly low return to us, but there is no reason to doubt its general correctness. When only 6 per cent. is deducted for seed, a return is left of £260,000,000. In all for this favourable year, adding a liberal amount for manufactures and every contingency, it is impossible to run the total above £340,000,000. Taking account, therefore, of the terribly low returns recently made manifest in Madras, Bombay, and other parts of India, sometimes not exceeding 10*s.* an acre, we may go back to the figures £300,000,000, with the assurance that the average produce of all India is not being undervalued.

Admitting then this £300,000,000 as a standard, it appears that the gross produce of 190,000,000 people is not worth more than 31*s.* 6*d.* per head. To compare one country with another in matters of this kind is an altogether fallacious test of prosperity, and no stress whatever ought to be laid on this point; still it is worthy of remark that the average gross produce of the United Kingdom and

Ireland is commonly put at not less than £30 a head, and is probably considerably more. What is, however, more to the purpose, is how great a proportion of this 31*s.* 6*d.* is needed to provide the actual necessaries of life at the current rates of the country, or, in other words, what proportion of his own produce can the agricultural labourer or the peasant cultivator retain, exclusive of taxation, for the use of himself and his family.

It must not be overlooked, in considering this, that although 31*s.* 6*d.* is the average gross income, that sum by no means represents the amount which the bulk of the agricultural and labouring population can possibly secure when the richer and middle classes are provided for at a higher standard. Mr. Robertson has told us what luxury the honest pauper ryot of Madras would consider such living as that secured by the criminals in gaol, though this remark is applicable to the people of other countries than India, Madras, however, happens to be the most expensive province in India as regards the cost of feeding prisoners. Taking Bengal then to represent, as it does, the medium cost in the same year as that for which the above calculations are made,—a year anterior to the heavy scarcity of 1868-9 in Northern India and the succeeding famines,—we find the cost of feeding a prisoner alone comes to 28 rupees, or, making allowance for children, that the cost of feeding the population out of gaol on the same scale as in, would be per head 23 rupees, or 46*s.* Deducting what may be pleased for extravagance and bad management, this still leaves a startling deficiency between 31*s.* 6*d.* and the gaol rate of nourishment, especially when it is considered that as yet no deduction has been made for the sustenance of bullocks, the cost of clothing, repairs to implements, house, etc., or for taxation.

Thus, even if the population engaged in agricultural labour, and other occupations incidental to cultivation of the soil, amounting altogether to fully 160,000,000 out of 190,000,000, were to retain all their produce, they would not be over-nourished or have much chance of saving.* Provision for a bad season becomes almost, if not quite, impossible. Ryots and labourers are living from hand to mouth over the greater part of India, and even so on very insufficient food. It serves to confirm this view that the wages of unskilled labour in districts remote from the railroads are still from 1½*d.* to 4*d.* a day for uncertain employment, whilst officials state that prices have risen.

Now the total revenue of India for the year 1876, which was not a famine year, was £51,310,063. The amount of this which is raised by taxation taken absolutely out of the pockets of the people, is as follows :—

Land Revenue	£21,500,000
Excise	2,500,000
Salt	6,240,000
Stamps	2,830,000
Customs	2,720,000
Total	£35,790,000

* "The mass of the people of India are so miserably poor that they have barely the means of subsistence; it is as much as a

Or, in round figures, £36,000,000. The remainder is made up from the opium revenue, tributes from native states, departmental payments, etc., which do not come from the people. The opium alone produces over £8,000,000 gross, and more than £6,000,000 net. This £36,000,000 apportioned per head of population is 3*s.* 9½*d.* each; truly, to all appearance, a ridiculously small sum. But it reduces the 31*s.* 6*d.*, which, as we have already seen, does not suffice to supply the necessaries of life, to 27*s.* 9*d.*; and 3*s.* 9½*d.*, or a little over 12 per cent., is, on this calculation, taken from the people for purposes of government. It is often urged that the £21,500,000 of land revenue is really rent, which is taken by the Government instead of by the landowners in other countries, and ought not to be considered as taxation. But rent paid to landowners is a portion of the produce of the soil taken and used on the spot: our rent is used in a very different way; and besides, what has now to be considered is the amount actually taken from the people out of their total small gross produce. It amounts then to 12 per cent., exclusive of the very heavy local cesses and muncipal rates, which have been increased £4,000,000 even since 1870, and now amount to £13,000,000, or more than an additional 4 per cent. for the whole of India. It will, therefore, in all likelihood, be within the mark if we put the total taxation of India, imperial and provincial, etc., at 16 per cent. on the gross income, or 5*s.* per head of population.

man can do to feed his family or to half feed them, let alone spending money on what you would call luxuries or conveniences."—*Lord Lawrence.*

In 1857 the heads of taxation similar to those already given above for 1876 were :—

Land Revenue	£17,720,000
Excise	1,000,000
Salt	2,680,000
Stamps	620,000
Customs	2,090,000
Total	£24,110,000

The amount of Imperial taxation twenty years ago was therefore, in round figures, £24,000,000, or as nearly as possible 2*s.* 6*d.* per head of population. The increase of £12,000,000 directly levied from the people comes almost entirely out of the pockets of the cultivators ; the additional £4,000,000 of the land revenue certainly does, and the greater part of the increase of the salt, stamps, and excise is derived from the same source.* Moreover, as local and municipal cesses were then almost unknown, it will scarcely be an exaggeration to say that the total weight of taxation to-day is as nearly as possible twice what it was twenty years ago, or £50,000,000 to £25,000,000. Thus the extra 2*s.* 6*d.* of Imperial and local taxation imposed per head in addition since the East India Company gave up the government amounts to 12*s.* 6*d.* in a family of five persons, an amount quite sufficient to make a material difference in the well-being of a family whose total gross income on our favourable hypothesis would only reach a little more than £7 17*s.* ;

* It will be observed that the chief weight of the taxation falls on the cultivators in any case. The whole land revenue is raised from them, £21,500,000, and they certainly pay their full proportion of other taxes.

whilst the imperial taxation alone at 3*s.* 9½*d.* a head amounts to nearly £1 on the same trifling family income.

I again state here what I have stated before, that this taxation so increased is levied from a people who are becoming poorer and poorer, and consequently is becoming more and more crushing in proportion to their means. Wherever the Government examines into the circumstances of a particular district, there this same appalling fact is found, that, so far from becoming richer, the ryots are losing what little means they had, and are falling fast bound into the grip of the usurers. The condition of the ryots in the Deccan is not exceptional, as the following extracts show. "The Calcutta Missionary Conference dwelt on the miserable, abject condition of the Bengal ryots, and there is evidence that they suffer many things, and are often in want of absolute necessaries. As a rule, they are comparatively better off in eastern Bengal and worse off in the west; the rates of wagesb eing higher in the east, and food cheaper, while rents are screwed up to a rack-rent pitch and light in comparison to the productiveness of the soil, and the remunerative character of their special crop—jute. In the west, and in Behar and Orissam, any labourers supplement home means by going to other parts of the country for temporary service and labour. In Burdwan the people are poorer than elsewhere, and the people of Assam, judged by an Indian standard, are very well off.

"In the North-West Provinces the wages of agricultural labour have hardly varied at all since the early part of this century; *and after the payment of the rent the margin left for the cultivator's subsistence is less than the value of the labour he has expended on his land.* The wages of a labourer in the ploughing season furnish him with fifty ounces of *behjur*, a compound of barley and peas, of which about forty-six ounces are nutritious. In the digging and weeding season he only gets thirty-four ounces, but sometimes his wife earns enough for twenty-five ounces more. He only tastes salt two or three times a week. Many live on a coarse grain called *kesari*, which is most unwholesome, and produces loin palsy. The small tenant farmers only get about the same amount of *behjur*, although they can have salt daily. This extreme poverty among the agricultural population is one of the reasons which makes any improvement in farming and cultivation so difficult."—"Moral and Material Progress of India," 1872-73. Read also the sentences which immediately follow with relation to wages and prices of food in other parts of India.

"A subject which has attracted much serious attention in connection with the administration of the land is the alleged indebtedness of the cultivating classes, with the result that their ancestral estates are gradually passing out of their hands through heavy mortgages and compulsory sales. This is reported to be the case in the Bombay Presidency, the Punjab, North-West Provinces, Oude, and Central provinces."—Moral and Material Progress of India, 1873-74. Why "alleged"? These are *official* reports stating definite facts in relation to a very wide extent of country, containing tens of millions of people. If they are not to be relied upon, what evidence have we got? Natives are not even listened to. Mr. Robertson vouches for the same state of things in Coimbatore, and the Famine Reports on Madras confirm his remarks in regard to many other districts in that province. There are 16,000,000 pauper ryots in Madras alone!

In the North-West Provinces Mr. Halsey says in regard to Cawnpore: "I assert that the abject poverty of the average cultivator of this district is beyond the belief of any one who has not seen it. He is simply a slave to the soil, to the zemindar, to the usurer, and to the Government. . . . The normal state of between three-fourths and four-fifths of the cultivators of this district is as I have above shown." The total gross produce of the North-West Provinces, as analysed by the native writer, whose figures have been quoted already, is hardly 27*s.* a head. Nor is this all by any means. There is distinct evidence that between 1860-61, the period of the great famine on which Colonel Baird Smith reported, and the present date, the average standard of comfort and amount of income per family has greatly declined. On the very first symptom of scarcity in these provinces thousands immediately died or came upon the hands of the Government. The pauper population here, too, is rivalling in numbers that of Madras.

In the Central Provinces we find precisely the same conditions, and Mr. W. G. Pedder, no alarmist, we may be very sure, says: "The people, if an almost universal consensus of opinion may be relied on, are rapidly going from bad to worse under our rule. This is a most serious question, and one well deserving the attention of the Government." Orissa has also been reduced even below what was the standard prior to the terrible famine in 1866. What the condition of the people was there at that time may be learned from the evidence of Mr. Geddes before the Indian Finance Committee of the House of Commons, from the report on the famine, and from the correspondence which took place at the time in India and England. The ryots were in the hands of the zemindars and shroffs, and were wholly unable to stand against the effects of one bad season. Orissa has become also greatly poorer owing to that famine and the increased taxation. Some parts of Bengal are better off, but others are worse still.

Thus, wherever officials look into the matter and speak their minds, increasing impoverishment is found. Yet, as Colonel Baird Smith says, "In India we all know very well that when the agricultural class is weak the weakness of all the other sections of the community is the inevitable consequence." Is it not an extraordinary thing that in the face of such circumstances the Government should persistently refuse to listen to natives? Only three native witnesses have been examined in England in this generation with regard to the affairs of their own country. Two of these predicted precisely what occurred afterwards in one district, and gave a most significant warning of the fate that was likely to befall the whole of our Indian Empire.

But when this terrible state of affairs is insisted

upon, and the absolute certainty of a general collapse is spoken of, many smile and point to the vastly increasing trade of British India as quite conclusive of the prosperity of the country. In commenting on the Indian Budget this is the common tone of those who support the present policy, and it is thought a sufficient answer to warnings of the danger of perpetual and ever-increasing deficits to talk of a total export and import trade considerably in excess of £100,000,000.

Before dealing with this unfortunate mistake, there is the effect of the drain upon India for payment of the home charges to be taken account of. These amounted in 1857, and generally under the East India Company's rule, to about £3,000,000, apart from remittances by private individuals, officers of the army, loot, etc. In the twenty years from 1857 to 1876 India paid home charges to the amount of £270,000,000 at the very lowest estimate. As this was almost all for unremunerative expenditure in a foreign country, we are able to judge what a drag this alone must have been upon such a poor country. Can we reasonably contend that this expenditure of the proceeds of Indian poverty in the shape of interest, army disbursements, an engineering college, etc., is compensated by the public works and the increased security under our rule? It is to be feared not. At any rate, the home charges for 1877-78 amounted to £16,500,000. Thus the depletion is progressing by leaps and bounds. No serious attempt whatever is made to check it, and yet it is scarcely necessary to show that a removal of £16,500,000 in 1877-78 from India to England is not only actually, but proportionately, a much more serious matter than a similar scale of home payments would have been in, say, 1873, seeing that, apart from the depletion of capital involved in the interval, there have been two great famines to impoverish the people.

Returning now to the trade of India, which is supposed to settle the question of her increasing wealth. Her exports are almost exclusively agricultural, and therefore it might be taken for granted that, as she does export agricultural produce so largely, the return from her soil, miserably small as its value appears, is, as with America, Australia, New Zealand, etc., far more than sufficient to support her cultivators, who form with the labourers three-fourths of the population, in at least moderate comfort and to maintain them well nourished. I have already shown that this is not the case, both *à priori* from the gross value of the produce as compared with the cost of the simplest necessaries of life, and then from the actual evidence of competent observers in various parts of India as to the almost incredible poverty of the mass of the people. The export, therefore, on which we pride ourselves, does not, so far as can be seen *in India*, proceed from a well-fed people.

How does it look from England? It is calculated by a gentleman who takes a most sanguine view of our position in India, and who would utterly scout the idea that the British connection, as at present managed, must prove fatal to that country, that "the amount of the annual earnings of Englishmen connected with India which are transmitted home cannot be less than £20,000,000, and he would be inclined to place it at a very much higher figure."* Admitting that even £10,000,000 are so sent home each year, what is the effect of this? The Englishmen who are working in India are remunerated for their labours by a proportion of the produce of the soil of that country. This remuneration is paid to them in money, but the money to pay them with and the money which they send to us here at home to keep their wives and families, to provide for the future, and to increase their pension,—which is another remittance already provided for in the home charges so far as officials are concerned,—is originally taken, of course, from the pockets of the people whom they govern or whose business they transact. Englishmen do not take up their abode in the country, do not now even live there very long together. In this we differ from all the foreign conquerors who have been in India before us, and the distinction is becoming more marked every year. Soldiers, civilians, engineers, all European agencies of every sort and kind, are not only paid out of the produce of India at a rate from three to eight times—people who have spent their lives in the country say in some cases from twenty to twenty-five times—as much as would have to be paid to natives, but the greater portion of this produce so paid for work done is sent to be used and expended in a foreign country, and thus India loses every way. This is an ordinary process going on every day.

A single illustration will suffice to show how the

* Mr. J. M. Maclean, M.P., a witness before the Committee of the House of Commons on East Indian Finance, 1873.

whole system of foreign agency works, and how absolutely necessary it is to keep it within very moderate limits. An English official in India receives say £3,000 a year, and saves one-third of his salary. In ten years he will have remitted to England the sum of £10,000 in addition to any pension which he might hereafter be entitled to. A native filling the same post at the same salary would undoubtedly save at least twice as much; but assuming that he saves only £1,000 a year, at the end of ten years he would have £10,000 in his hands for remunerative employment in India; his pension also would be spent in India. Thus the capital of India would be £10,000 larger in the one case than in the other, and the pension would be used to feed Indian mouths instead of foreign ones. One great object, therefore, for the future should be gradually to supplant Europeans by natives, at lower salaries if desired, in all save the very highest posts. These should be used merely for purposes of superintendence, to insure right principles of administration. Steps are being taken to give more employment to natives, but hitherto they have been very hesitating.

Now look at the trade figures for the twenty years:—The total exports and imports of India, from 1857 to 1876 inclusive, amount to £997,063,848 and £841,192,237 respectively. Discriminating between merchandise and bullion in the imports, we have merchandise to the value of £569,835,243 imported in that period, and £271,356,994 worth of bullion. Between 1857 and 1876 the total export and import trade together increased from

£55,000,000 to £103,000,000, or very nearly doubled. Nothing could be more satisfactory is the general verdict. Trade doubled—capital. Exports exceed imports—that is all right. Great inflow of bullion—the country *must* be getting richer.

But to estimate correctly the above figures, which are calculated at the Indian ports, it is obvious that at least 15 per cent. must be added to the exports for profit, etc., and that therefore the value of the imports to balance these exports should not be less than £1,145,000,000.* They were £841,000,000. Here is a discrepancy to start with of more than £300,000,000. Of the imports, however, £271,000,000 consisted of bullion. Now of this £271,000,000, certainly not less than £120,000,000 represents the proceeds of loans raised or guaranteed by Government, and brought into India as a borrowed fund, wherewith to pay the wages of labourers, engineers, etc., engaged on public works. It is treasure which has been borrowed for a definite period, which is still owing, and which has to be repaid. This, therefore, is no trade import.

We have thus the original disparity of more than £300,000,000 plus £120,000,000 as the drain from India in the twenty years. That amounts to £420,000,000, or £21,000,000 a year. It would be easy to show that the actual drain is much greater than this when the opium profits, and the import of treasure to carry on the increased private business

* The reason for this is, that the estimate of value is made at the Indian ports, where freight, profit, and insurance are calculated in giving the value of the imports, but no such addition is made for the exports.

(which is also on loan), are taken into the account. The above figures are, however, sufficient to establish the principle for which I contend—that the export trade of India represents a most exhausting drain on the country.

Even leaving out the profit and taking no account of the opium monopoly, India has sustained a drain of nearly £280,000,000 in the twenty years. The exports for 1876-7 were £65,000,000, and the imports, exclusive of bullion, were £37,427,000, with bullion, nearly £49,000,000.

A further examination of the trade and the conditions under which it is carried on—always bearing in mind that if ever there existed a poor agricultural country in this world, India is that country—tends to remove what little ground for complacency is still left to us. Looking into the list of imports, we find that, with the exception of one large item, the greater portion of the import is for stores, etc., on European and Government account, and is therefore no demand by the population at all. That one large item is, of course, cotton. The import of cotton of various kinds into India in 1857 amounted to £6,000,000. Similar imports in 1876 amounted to £19,000,000, a subject doubtless for a good deal of congratulation to us. Whether the gain to India is quite so manifest is another thing. No doubt the cultivators get their scanty clothing cheaper than when they bought the native manufactures; but the destruction of those manufacturing industries, has that been entirely a gain to India? Unquestionably not. India paid to England in 1876 £13,000,000 for wages, profit, and freight, which in 1857 she paid to her own countrymen, less the price of the raw cotton ; and though the ryot gets his cotton cloth a little cheaper, there is nothing to show that he is any better clothed than he was twenty years ago, or is enabled to spend more upon dress—rather the contrary. Surely this is no evidence then that our trade is benefiting India. The workers in cotton industries whom our goods have displaced have had to seek their living elsewhere. They have not gone into fresh manufacturing industries, that is certain. It is almost beyond question that they and their families have been driven to agriculture, and if the operation of this cause could be traced, I have very little doubt it would be found that here is one great reason for the cultivation of waste lands of which we have heard so much. If India profits by the trade, if indeed she be not an enormous and an increasing loser by it, where is the evidence of well-being ? To that question we ever return.

"In the exports of course" will not perhaps be said quite so confidently as before this inquiry was commenced. When a trade can be shown to have depleted a country to the extent of at least £420,000,000 in twenty years—when it can be shown almost beyond the possibility of question that a poor agricultural population has been driven, with the action of that trade in full work, to cultivate yet poorer soils and to part with its few manufacturing industries—when we are obliged perforce to admit that the bulk of the people have less and less to fall back upon in a scarcity year—then an increasing export of food stuffs or other produce becomes a very sinister symptom.

What, once more, say English officials on the spot? That the cultivators must grow for export, must cultivate what is saleable for money in order to pay their taxes in money, and to satisfy the demands of the native usurers, who besides have, to all intents and purposes, a great proportion of the crops in their hands. The prospect of famine does not check the export, actual famine does not altogether stop it. In Orissa, though famine was seen to be coming upon them in 1865, food stuffs were exported from the province in order to get money to meet the Government demand. During the year 1877 the North-West Provinces exported grain largely, have been exporting grain up to this very time to Madras and England, though 300,000 people, according to thoroughly trustworthy testimony, died in those provinces of starvation during that period. The first thing to be met is the revenue and local charges, the next the soucar's usurious interest; provision of food for men and animals comes afterwards.

It should never be left out of mind that in India at this time millions of the ryots are growing wheat, cotton, seeds, and other exhausting crops, and send them away, because these alone will enable them to pay their way at all. They are themselves, nevertheless, eating less and less of worse food each year in spite, or rather by reason, of the increasing exports. In England, a rich country, we leave money to "fructify in the pockets of the people," and keep taxation low. In India, a very poor country, we want the money to fructify in the hands of Government and keep taxation high. The total export and import trade of India—and the trade of the native states with a population of 50,000,000 is included in the above returns—amounted, after all, to but 12*s.* per head of the population in 1876. It is not such a foreign trade as this, even assuming the largest rate of profit conceivable, that will restore India to wealth and prosperity. An increased Indian trade is very far indeed, under present circumstances, from being a make-weight against increased Indian taxation.

But still graver features may be noted. There is no reason to suppose that the soil of India is naturally poorer than that of any other land, nor is there any obvious cause why the return from the soil should be so low—why, indeed, it should not produce as largely as any other tropical country under good management. The variation of the seasons is more than compensated by the wonderful effect of warmth and sunshine in a good year. There is, however, grave reason to fear that in many districts the soil is being worse cultivated, or is going steadily through a process of deterioration; or sometimes one of these causes and sometimes the other, and not unfrequently both together, are at work. Undoubtedly exhausting crops are being grown to an extent previously unknown. What is taken out of the soil by such crops must be put back into it either by fallows, or by skiful rotation of crops, or by an extra supply of manures from some source outside of the particular land. Fallows have almost ceased in India, rotation of crops is at best very imperfect, and the supply of manure from bullocks depastured in waste lands has all but disappeared.

Here again the want of trustworthy agricultural statistics is to be deplored. But as to the imperfect cultivation compared with former times the evidence unfortunately seems only too conclusive.

The Indian peasantry depend for the cultivation of their soil upon bullocks A good supply of good bullocks, other things being equal, means good cultivation ; an insufficient supply of inferior bullocks means inferior cultivation, and this invariably. Now there are beyond all question fewer bullocks in India than there were. Lord Lawrence in his evidence, speaking from the result of forty years' experience in every capacity, gives it as his opinion that good cattle for any purpose are much more difficult to come by than they were, and this is the general statement of qualified observers. In one district in Madras, which, to all appearance, does not differ from others, tabulated statistics have been published, which show clearly that, owing to the breaking up of pasture, the taking in of waste lands, and other causes, the bullocks are fewer and of a far inferior and weaker breed. This process of deterioration is going on all over India, so far as can be judged. Everywhere it is a matter for remark that, whatever drawbacks there may be to native rule in other respects, the cattle in the native States are of a far finer quality and more numerous than in British territory. Under our *régime* all is order and security, more land is tilled, and the people ought to be better off, and have, of course, better cattle. But want of capital, absorption of waste land, and the murrains which Lord Lawrence attributes to the excessive price of salt under our system of taxation,—a system almost infinitely heavier on this particular item than was ever known under native rule,—have gradually lessened the numbers and enfeebled the breed even in good times; whilst the old Hindoo aversion to killing off the old and useless animals remains as strong as ever.

Famines, of course, tell strongly in the same direction. The cattle lost in Orissa were estimated at a value of £1,000,000. The sacrifice in Behar I have not been able to trace, but it must have been considerable. In the Madras famine it is officially calculated that fully 75 per cent. of the non-agricultural cattle died, and probably not less than 40 per cent. of the agricultural cattle shared the same fate. In spite of the most strenuous efforts made by the natives to save them,—for on their method of cultivation, deprived of bullocks, sheer starvation stares the ryots in the face,—in spite of using the thatch of their poor hovels for fodder, the deaths of cattle in 1876-77 alone, according to the Administration Report for that year, were 935,000, and as many in the other famine year. The deaths of cattle in the famine-stricken districts of Bombay stand in the same proportion.

This destruction of bullocks has perhaps been almost the most serious result, in the long run, of the six, some reckon eight, great famines which have afflicted India during the twenty years. Leaving manure entirely out of the question, we here have cultivation carried on by fewer and feebler beasts as well as by poorer and worse-nourished men. Need we look much further to understand how it is that famines are perpetuated under our rule? An impoverished people, an imperfect cultivation by fewer and weaker bullocks on a too often deteriorated soil, increased taxation, and, on the top of all, a drought. Allow this process to go on, the Government paying for the cost of saving the majority alive, and the State itself—which is, after all, but another name for the organised resources of the people—will rest upon a crowd of half-starved paupers. How will they be able to support one another in time of need?

Here, however, the railways and irrigation works of which we have heard so much, and which have positively given rise to two hostile parties of economical reformers,—the railway-builders and the irrigationists,—should come in to help us. Names of eloquent advocates of both methods rise unbidden to one's memory; and if half we have heard of their value were true, all that would have to be done would be to continue borrowing money for the purpose of constructing one or the other, or the two together. This is the opinion of Sir John Strachey, a recent Finance Minister, and of the Government of India, as well in England as in India. Public works, made from the proceeds of fresh taxation or fresh loans, are the great official panacea for famine now as heretofore. It is not even yet understood that the only means whereby a nation as a whole can provide against years of scarcity is by laying aside food out of years of plenty, or, which amounts to the same thing, saving the money obtained from the sales of surplus produce in one district or country, if surplus produce there be, to buy the surplus produce of another in case of need. Take away that reserve either for railway building, irrigation, or any other purpose, and scarcity deepens at once into famine. True, the railways did bring food from the North-West Provinces and the Punjab to Bombay and Madras; but the people had not the money to buy it with when it came. Therefore they starved.

To take nevertheless the cost of the Indian railways and their work. According to Sir Juland Danvers, the 5,900 miles of guaranteed lines actually cost, up to 1877, £95,200,000 on capital account; and the £28,000,000 advanced for guaranteed interest to the 31st December, 1876. We thus arrive at a grand total of over £130,000,000 in round figures as the cost of, say, 6,000 miles of railway, or at the rate of £21,000 a mile. £21,000 a mile for railroads in the poorest agricultural country in the world! Even so the value of the land and other Government grants is not reckoned. Thus, leaving aside the capital account as purely English, we find that £28,000,000 of Indian money had been spent on these guaranteed railways, which only earned their interest last year for the first time since their construction, because of the enormous transport necessitated by the famine. The State railways, on which £17,000,000 had been spent, are in a yet worse case; they do not earn 1 per cent. interest on the money they have cost. Every unfortunate ryot who has had to borrow an additional five or ten or twenty rupees of the native moneylender, at 24, 40, 60 per cent., in order to pay extra taxation, every poor famine-stricken creature whom that small sum might have tided over to a better day, has bitter reason to ask whether this is what Europeans mean by development—whether these are the highest calculations of English finance.

The story of our irrigation works tells nearly the same sad tale. Here again millions have been squandered—squandered needlessly with wholly inadequate results. The only works which have been even partially successful are those which have supplemented or restored old native systems of wells, tanks, and anicuts, or cautiously attempted new works on the same lines. Though the Indian Government has been asked over and over again to give accurate accounts of the returns of these irrigation works, it has never yet done so. According to those appended to the Return of East India Finance and Revenue Accounts, a sum of £16,000,000 has been spent; and yet, in spite of cultivators having in many instances been forced to take and pay for water which they do not want, there is a dead loss on the working. That the cultivators in the immediate neighbourhood of these irrigation works, or those close to the railroads, may be benefited by such outlay, is quite possible; but they are so at the expense of the great mass of the people, who have been still further impoverished by the additional taxation necessitated to pay the interest charges on these costly failures.

Irrigation water will not run uphill, nor always be at hand in a year of drought; railways will not put back that money into the pockets of the cultivators which has been drained away from them, or which they have been forced to run into debt for at usurious interest; further borrowing to construct public works which, so far as can be judged now, are likely to turn out no better than their precursors, is most dangerous: in India improvements ought to be made out of savings from a *light* taxation instead of out of borrowing (which may impose a permanent charge on the country through any miscalculation), or by increasing an already *heavy* taxation for the like purpose. Lord Salisbury saw all this clearly enough, but unfortunately both for England and for India he has not had the courage of his opinions. Speaking at Bradford in 1877, he, as Secretary of State for India, said:—

"We must not look to irrigation as an extensive remedy against famine. If we expend money rashly upon irrigation works which will not pay, and cannot be used by the inhabitants, the interest of that money must be found out of taxes which must in the main be levied on the peasant; and the end would be that in order to save him from famine which comes [upon him individually] once in twenty years, we should crush him under an increased burden of taxes which comes upon him every year. . . . Now depend upon it the only true remedy against famine and scarcity is the frugality of the people. The people ought in years of plenty to make money enough to lay up against these times of famine, and it is to the improvement of their social and moral condition, it is to this rather than to any great and passionate expenditure on public works, that I should look for a remedy."

How severe a criticism is this speech of Lord Salisbury's on the policy now definitely adopted and sanctioned by the Home Government!

Finance is indeed the key to Indian prosperity—nay, it is the door of the building, or rather the whole house itself. The bearing of what has gone before on the Indian Budget is therefore obvious. We have to deal with an inelastic revenue. The grand total of the actual revenue for 1876-77 is indeed given as £55,995,785 as against £51,310,063 for 1875-76, but this apparent increase is obtained by the addition of certain figures to both sides of the account. The facts, of course, are not changed in the least by this process. The revenue for 1877-78 is put at £58,635,472 on the same basis. Now the deficit for 1876-77, including Public Works Extraordinary, now called Productive Public Work Capital Expenditure,—works, as we have seen, very far from "productive" hitherto in any natural sense, and entailing a loss in working of over £1,100,000 that year,—amounted to just £6,000,000; in round figures the deficit for 1877-78 was £8,200,000, and the deficit for 1878-79 estimated at over £2,000,000. Thus we have here an accumulated deficit in the three years of more than £16,000,000 on a stationary revenue. Sir John Strachey, in his Budget statements at Calcutta, reckoned the total cost of the Bengal and Madras famines at £16,000,000, imposing, as he said, a permanent extra yearly charge upon India of no less a sum than £640,000.

Now it seems almost incredible that, in the

face of this and of the result of public works expenditure up to the present time, the Government in India and at home should positively continue to raise £1,500,000 additional taxation from the impoverished inhabitants of India, adding to their already crushing impost of 5*s.* a head on a total gross produce (it is much less during late years) of 31*s.* 6*d.* to build yet more public works. Yet so it is.

As to the extent to which this terrible mania is already carried, it may be pointed out that, apart from the loss of over £1,100,000 on working expenses and interest in 1876-77 on these "productive" public works already spoken of, there was spent a total amount in that year of no less than £7,300,000 on public works ordinary and extraordinary; or, adding the £1,100,000, an amount of £8,400,000 and more represents the money swept away by this single item in a year of most frightful suffering for millions of the people. The manner in which the additional £1,500,000 is to be obtained is even more objectionable than the purpose to which, when raised, it is to be applied. It is to be raised from the ryots and small traders in the towns by increased land cesses, and a license tax because—but Sir John Strachey must really speak for himself. Hear what he said in his speech at Calcutta on the 27th December, 1877:—

"There is certainly no reason in the condition of the agricultural classes why they should not bear their share of any necessary fresh taxation for the purpose of protecting themselves and the country against famine. . . . In times of famine no large proportion of these [the upper classes] come upon the relief which the Government has to administer. The poorer field labourers in the villages and the poorer members of the trading and industrial classes in the towns are the first section of the population which suffers; and even when famine is at its height the mass of the people receiving relief are field labourers, petty ryots, and artisans. Very few priests, and lawyers, and schoolmasters, and people with fixed incomes actually demand Government relief, although they may feel sorely the pressure of famine prices. This class, with more or less fixed incomes, then, although we cannot relieve it, will have no fresh burdens imposed upon it by the measures which we now desire to take."

That is to say, the only really well-to-do classes in India, the European officials, officers, and professional men, are shielded from any additional taxation, and the wealthy native traders, and merchants, and bankers, who alone benefit by the trade of the famines, are lightly taxed, because they never suffer from famine or lose their substance; but the ryots and small hawkers are taxed because they feel the pressure of scarcity immediately. Why, at this rate, all the poor-rates in Great Britain would be raised from the agricultural and artisan classes, and they would be taxed an additional amount in an exceptionally bad year. To tax the miserably poor population of India still more at such a time to build more public works when already the peasants are insufficiently fed and are wholly unable to exercise that "frugality" in a year of plenty which, Lord Salisbury rightly urges, is the only remedy for famine—to tax them so, I say, is but to hurry on and render more utterly hopeless that catastrophe which all must be anxious to avert.

In Bombay and Madras the already almost prohibitive salt-tax was raised 40 per cent. A tax on a necessary of life to the people is increased in that ratio at the time of their direst need. There is not an official in these provinces who would affirm that even at the old prices the poorer natives could afford enough of this absolute necessary. If there is one fact which has been made more clear than another, it is that the salt-tax, as at present levied, is injurious to the health of the people, damaging to their cattle, and that it positively cuts at the root of many essential industries. Sir John Strachey himself spoke in 1877 strongly of the necessity, the pressing necessity, of reducing the salt-tax; in 1878 he raised it to a starving population. But the salt-tax has been lowered in Bengal, which at present, owing to the permanent settlement over a great portion of the province, is comparatively the most prosperous part of India; but the Customs Line has been removed, but no addition has been made to the local cesses in southern India. This is so, and furthermore, by the obviously too low estimate of the Government of India itself, 1,400,000 people died from actual starvation in southern India, more than 50 per cent. of the cattle perished in many districts, and the bulk of the population, utterly destitute to-day, can, under the most favourable circumstances, hope for no more than the barest subsistence to-morrow. Droughts and scarcities there must ever be, death and disease no Government can prevent, but we are aggravating every ill that flesh is heir to by the policy still in favour in Calcutta and in London.

But the revenue of India itself when collected is subject to such terrible chances, that at all times the closest watching and economy are needed. To say nothing of the opium revenue, which, though more to be relied upon than some think, is not a good item on which to base the stability of each successive budget to the amount of at least a net £6,000,000, we have in future to encounter a great and increasing loss by exchange on the home charges to the amount of an estimated £3,000,000 for the year 1878-79. This no one has yet even proposed to deal with. Years hence, perhaps, it will be thought strange that an empire which received £50,000,000 of its revenue in silver should have been anxious and even eager to sécure the demonetisation of that metal.

But we must take the facts as they are, and they are awkward enough. For the total net revenue of India to supply all needs, when cost of collection is deducted, is placed by Sir John Strachey himself at a sum not exceeding £40,000,000. Out of this the army, including marine and incidental charges for military purposes, must be taken to cost little less than £19,000,000. The interest on the debt is £5,400,000. Absentee allowances, superannuation payments, and political agencies amount to over £2,500,000, and when to these items is added the loss by exchange and loss on "productive works," it is manifest that the £40,000,000 leaves but little for the administration—without any talk of the improvement—of 190,000,000 people.

The cost of the army is so enormous that this disbursement alone is deserving of special notice. Lord Canning, speaking after the Mutiny, said that the whole military charges for India ought not to exceed £12,500,000; and there can be little doubt that if the old Indian army were re-established as a portion of the Imperial forces, and proper reforms introduced in the service, this sum would fully suffice to support at least our present force. As it is, including the cost of military works, etc., the amount falls not far short of the figures named before, or £19,000,000. During the fifteen years 1863-1878 also the increase in the home military charges alone has been quite alarming. In 1862-63 the home military charges for 75,899 men serving in India amounted to £2,139,205. or a little more than £28 3*s.* a head. In 1877-78 the home military charges amounted to no less than £4,168,600, though the numbers have been decreased by 13,000, and the European force at the latter date was 62,652 men. This shows a charge per head of over £66, or more than two and one-third times the cost in 1863. During the last ten years of the Company's rule the average recruiting charge was £19 14*s.* 10¼*d.* per man; in 1878 it was £79 3*s.* 10*d.* per man, the cost having increased fourfold. The more narrowly the details of these charges are examined into, the more extravagant and unjust do they appear. Such reckless expenditure soon necessitates fresh loans from

England. Further borrowing, however, will soon become impossible at present rates. Investors must soon appreciate the real state of affairs—the sooner the better for India. The debt in 1878 was over £127,000,000, putting aside the guaranteed railways; and still we borrow on.*

National bankruptcy is a very ugly phrase, but it surely rests with those who impose extra taxation in a famine year to show that the fast increasing uneasiness is unfounded, and that their own figures, which show how near the final collapse of the Indian finances under present management must really be, are utterly fallacious. During the twenty years also we had perfect peace. How long may that continue? Yet even with this profound peace sixteen out of the twenty years have been years of deficit, and in the meantime Imperial and local taxation has been doubled.

It is needless to go further. I can only repeat that the natives of India are growing poorer and poorer; that taxation is not only actually but relatively far heavier; that each successive scarcity widens the area of impoverishment, and renders famines more frequent; that most of the trade is but an index to the poverty and crushing over-taxation of the people; that a highly-organised foreign rule constitutes by itself a most terrible drain

* "We are an alien power ruling at an enormous disadvantage, principally by force of character and administrative skill. As long as the natives of Hindustan believe that whatever power might follow us, native or European, will tax them more heavily than we do, we are safe. Should the other feeling prevail, we shall lose our hold on the country."—HUNTER's "Life of Lord Mayo," vol. ii., p. 286.

upon the country; and that all the railways and irrigation works on the planet, if concentrated in India at the cost of the peasantry, would but serve to hasten the inevitable catastrophe. The remedies are at hand, but it will take us five-and-twenty years at least of continuous and unremitting statesmanship to repair the blunders we have committed. Reduced expenditure on the army, suspension of public works, the steady substitution of natives for Europeans in the government and administration, a really light permanent settlement in every part of India, and lowering of taxation of every description, at any rate for the present—these are a few of the steps which have become absclutely essential.

From the narrowest view of self-interest this is to our advantage. All agree that, so long as the agricultural class is well affected to us, they will fight on our side, and we can easily maintain our rule; but let them become discontented, as they are becoming discontented now, and no man can tell what it would cost us in men and money to hold the country. To say that this or that reform cannot be carried out, means simply that we prefer to postpone the day of reckoning, which will be all the more terrible for India and for us when it comes.

Furthermore, the ryots of India would be our best customers if only we would leave the most thrifty, patient, hard-working peasantry in the world the means to improve their own condition. Their demand now for our manufactured goods is at the outside 2*s.* 6*d.* a head, though, to secure this, we have displaced nearly all the native industries. A demand of even £1 a head for English goods would still be trifling by the side of that of the population of our great free-governed colonies, but would secure us here alone an active export of £190,000,000 a year. There would be no need to grumble about fresh markets then. Our best markets are with our own people, and their continuous impoverishment must tell even on their present insignificant purchases. Already we seem to have reached the extreme limit of their buying capacity, and the only encouraging feature for India is that she seems once more on the road to supplying her own, or a portion of her own necessities. On the grounds, therefore, both of national security and national wealth, the present extravagant and dangerous, though doubtless thoroughly well-meaning, policy must be abandoned.

Here, if anywhere, it behoves us to rise to the level of our vast responsibilities. This matter of the impoverishment and decay of India is no affair of this party or of that, of regard for one man or for the other. It is a question which deeply concerns every Englishman among us, and can only be adequately handled by the strenuous exertions of all. The situation in India is one which must be dealt with immediately, and yet upon sound principles which will stand the test of years. Continuity of statesmanship,—statesmanship of the highest order, which grasps details, but can surely apply great principles,—this, if ever, is called for at this most critical juncture. The widest publicity, the most implicit confidence in the people, would but serve to strengthen the hands of the Minister who attempted courageously to discharge so honourable a duty ; for it is in seasons of real difficulty and danger that his countrymen have always shown the highest capacity, and have most earnestly supported those who strive to avert the disasters which may threaten the community.

II.

CONTROVERSY.

We have thus seen that if a large amount of official evidence and the testimony of facts and figures are deserving of credit, the people of India, as a whole, are getting poorer and poorer under our administration. Our public works, on which such enormous sums of money were expended, have been, and even still are, carried on at a dead loss to the population; and the unfortunate tax-payers are too frequently forced to borrow at usurious rates to pay the interest which the Government has guaranteed on these unprofitable investments. This by itself is a very serious matter where the bulk of the people are so miserably poor.

Famines have proved conclusively that the gravest poverty exists in almost every district. During the twenty years dealt with they were very numerous, and the plan which is now adopted, of making the poorer classes of one province pay to keep alive the mass of the famine-stricken people in another,—this process being reversed when the former suffer in turn,—cannot fail in the end to bring about a terrible catastrophe. For, as has already been shown, the soil of India is undergoing steady deterioration in many districts, owing to a variety of causes. The liability to famine is therefore increasing, whilst the power to support dearth is becoming less. Consequently droughts that formerly produced only a scarcity, now result in wholesale sacrifice of population and animals.

As to taxation, it has undoubtedly increased largely since the East India Company's rule, and in the opinion of men of unquestioned authority is now so heavy upon the great mass of the inhabitants, that any additions to the present burdens would not only be harmful to the people, but positively dangerous to the continuance of our rule. Above all, the constant drain from India due to a foreign administration, on account of the enormous home charges and excessive cost of European agency, renders the accumulation of capital almost out of the question, and this—the gravest and, from some points of view, most hopeless feature in the whole story of our connection with the country—is growing at an increasingly rapid rate. Such, in brief, is a summary of the situation. A very poor people heavily taxed in proportion to their means, suffering constantly from scarcities which the lack of savings converts into famine, a deteriorated soil, unprofitable public works, and over all a constant drain of tribute to a foreign state almost sufficient of itself to account for the growing impoverishment.

There were printed three official answers to the foregoing chapter which contained these statements, and gave the evidence on which they were based. One of these, by Sir Erskine Perry, was published in December 1878 in the *Nineteenth Century*, another by Mr. John Morley, written upon materials furnished by Sir John Strachey and other leading Indian officials, appeared in the *Fortnightly Review* for the same month, and a third official statement was put forward anonymously in *Fraser's Magazine*, likewise in December. Now it is at least certain that we have in these three articles the full force of the official case. Sir Erskine Perry was a member of the Indian Council, and had been connected with India, in one capacity or another, for nearly forty years. Sir John Strachey was then the Finance Minister, and he had risen to that important office through all the different grades of the Indian Civil Service. "D.," the writer in *Fraser*, is likewise an official. As, also, two full months elapsed, there was plenty of time to lay the India Office under contribution to prove conclusively that increasing prosperity which would completely overthrow the whole argument on the other side.

But whatever else has been shaken, certainly the general impoverishment of the people is admitted only too fully.

It is worthy of remark also that not one of these writers touched the origin and history of famines, save in the most perfunctory way. If, as I contend is the case, the twenty years—1858 to 1878—were chiefly remarkable for the number and the severity of the famines in various parts of India—if, as is admitted by Sir John Strachey himself, the cost of providing against these recurrent misfortunes must be regarded as a permanent charge against Indian finance—if they impoverish and weaken not only the population which they decimate, but those portions of the country which contribute to support the sufferers, surely it was the business of one at least of these official apologists to place on record his opinion as to the unprecedented frequency of these terrible events. What had Sir Erskine Perry to say to this? Not a word. What explanation did Mr. John Morley offer, in his forcible and lucid style, of so fatal an outcome of our system of government? The subject did not interest either himself or his official *clientèle.* At any rate, not two sentences are devoted to the matter. "D." is equally reticent, though he piles up figures on minor points with wearisome assiduity.

Surely then we have here a very significant and sinister omission. Consider this: Although eleven millions sterling are now put as the cost of the famine in southern India; although the Government, when it appreciated the facts, strained every nerve to save the people, yet, according to the calculations of the official statisticians themselves, 1,400,000 individuals perished of actual starvation in that great dearth. Other enumerations, made by men who had nothing whatever to gain by exceeding the truth, run the total up to at least 5,000,000 in Madras and Mysore alone. Nor should it be forgotten that this occurred under circumstances more than ordinarily favourable to the saving of life. There was no total loss of crop, except over a small area, and the means of communication were exceptionally good. To quote Lord Lytton: "There are several railway lines in the south of India; a number of seaports are available on the east and west coasts; Madras

6

possesses a better system of metalled and bridged roads than any part of India; much of the Bombay and Mysore country is also well supplied with roads. There was thus every facility for the free action of private trade." But, all this notwithstanding, the result was that loss of life which we all deplore.

Here, then, I say, are circumstances which absolutely demanded consideration at the hands of my critics. What better evidence of increasing poverty can be given than that hundreds of thousands or millions of men should die of starvation, with plenty of food to be had for those who could afford to buy it? What more deadly condemnation of our present system than that the unequalled exertions of the Government, seconded by the resources of private traders, could produce no better result? Take and read the famine reports, examine the arguments of the Madras Government against demanding "arrears of revenue" from men who could barely keep body and soul together, and then again consider how it comes about that men of name and reputation, who are so fully satisfied with our existing administration that they can afford to strengthen their case with misstatement and ridicule, deliberately turn aside from such terrible blots as these.

Here, however, I would say that I desire to reform, not to destroy, to improve, and not to uproot. A foreign Government always works at a great disadvantage, but under favourable conditions it may possibly confer benefits which outweigh its drawbacks. Our position in India is such that we cannot leave it at once consistently with fairness either to ourselves or to the native population; but we can at least lessen the burden which falls upon our fellow-subjects, and, by altering that which is proved to be objectionable in our management, try to render our connection with the country a gain to both parties. This, however, is no easy matter, and the vested interests, which day by day grow stronger, render the application of the only possible remedies more and more difficult.

I turn now to what has been urged against the general line of my argument. Before, however, dealing with such criticisms in detail, it may be well to note how far the official views are in accordance with those which I have expressed. I urged that the cultivating class of India is excessively poor, that—owing chiefly to the want of capital—it is getting poorer, and that our attempts to improve matters have too often served but to aggravate the original evil. Now listen to Sir Erskine Perry: he resided in India for many years, and generally devoted his vacations to travelling all over the country, "mostly at a foot's pace." Better evidence could not be. Here it is:—

"The dense population, amounting in its more fertile parts to six and seven hundred per square mile, is almost exclusively occupied in agricultural pursuits. But the land of India has been farmed from time immemorial by men entirely without capital. A farmer in this country has little chance of success unless he can supply a capital of £10 to £20 an acre. If English farms were cultivated by men as deficient in capital as the Indian ryots, they would all be thrown on the parish in a year or two. The founder of a Hindu village may, by the aid of his brethren and friends, have strength enough to break up the jungle, dig a well, and, with a few rupees in his pocket, he may purchase seed for the few acres he can bring under the plough. If a favourable harvest ensue, he has a large surplus, out of which he pays the *jamma* or rent to Government. But, on the first failure of the periodical rains, his withered crops disappear; he has no capital wherewith to meet the Government demand, to obtain food for his family and stock, or to purchase seed for the coming year. To meet all these wants he must have recourse to the village moneylender—[whence, by the way, did he get his capital?]—who has always formed as indispensable a member of a Hindu agricultural community as the ploughman himself."

Surely a very "sensational" statement this! No picture that I have painted of the poverty of the cultivator at all exceeds it in gloom. In what manner, however, have we set about improving the condition of these poverty-stricken people? Hear Sir Erskine again:—

"Every Englishman in office in India has great powers, and every Englishman—as the late Lord Lytton once observed to me—is in heart a reformer. His native energy will not enable him to sit still with his hands before him. He must be improving something. The tendency of the English official in India is to over-reform, to introduce what he may deem improvements, but which turn out egregious failures, and this, be it observed, amongst the most conservative people of the world. Some of the most carefully devised schemes for native improvement have culminated in native deterioration."

Why, what have we here? A denunciation of our practice of continuous reformation, irrespective of native habits and customs, and a distinct statement that many such schemes as have found favour with officials have but culminated in "native deterioration." But once more:—

"Every ardent administrator desires improvements in his own department; roads, railways, canals, irrigation, improved courts of justice, more efficient police, all find earnest advocates in the higher places of government. But improved administration is always costly, and requires additional taxation. I fear those in authority too often forget that the wisest rulers of a despotic Government have always abstained from laying fresh burdens on the people. It is, in fact, the chief merit of such a Government that the taxes are ordinarily light, and are such as are familiarised by old usage. New taxes, imposed without the will or any appeal to the judgment of the people, create the most dangerous kind of disaffection. But if this is true generally, it is especially true in India, where the population is extremely poor, and where hitherto the financier has not been enabled to make the rich contribute their due quota to the revenue of the country."

Now these remarks were made, let it be remembered, by a member of the Council of India in reply to a writer who has not and did not pretend to have any acquaintance with India, other than could be derived from books and papers, and information obtained at secondhand. They seem serious enough; for we are told of ryots without capital vexed with improvements that do not answer, and ground down by excessive taxation, against which there is no appeal. Is not this a state of affairs which, on any showing, it behoves the English people to look into for themselves? Is not this a matter where strenuous and continual exertion on the part of all of us can alone be of any avail?

Even so the gravest point is barely touched upon. This is the want of capital. On that all are agreed. The agriculturist has no capital, or very little, and, so far as can be judged, the little he has does not tend to increase. There is indeed but too much reason to believe that the entire capital of India, whether for the improvement of agriculture or for any other purpose, is dwindling year by year. The economical drain which has been so often disputed, and on many occasions entirely denied, has been admitted by the late Finance Minister of India, Sir John Strachey himself, to the amount of £20,000,000. It is reckoned by others, who have closely studied the subject, at a much larger sum.

But even those figures are surely sufficient to cause deep alarm to all who consider that the growing welfare of India is not only desirable from the point of view of humanity, but because it would beyond question give more employment to our own people at home. £20,000,000 taken out of India for England, means that the whole of the land revenue of our territory leaves the country—means that nearly one-third of the total exports of 190,000,000 people meets with no return. Can we wonder that the yearly drain of such a sum from so poor a country as Sir Erskine Perry describes has the effect of reducing the unfortunate cultivators and labourers to a lower and yet lower state of poverty and hopelessness? We cannot; and "D." admits what must be the natural consequences of the mistaken attempts at improvement, the continuous denudation of forests, and the over-Europeanising of the administration—the probable deterioration of the soil over large portions of India. What these various admissions amount to, what these now established facts portend, will appear in the following pages.

In endeavouring to show the poverty of the people of India as compared with the condition of the people of Great Britain, the sum of £300,000,000 was taken, with the sanction, as noticed above, of two of the highest official authorities, to represent the total gross income of 190,000,000 inhabitants; and the able writer in the *Quarterly Review* for January 1871 arrives at pretty nearly the same figures by an entirely independent route. Upon this single point, which is but one out of many that tell in the same direction, the main stress of the official argument has been laid. Sir James Caird—so Sir Erskine Perry and Mr. John Morley triumphantly insisted—at once proved, as "C." in the *Times*, that I was utterly wrong, and my "pessimist" views were entirely incorrect, inasmuch as I had "committed the error of arguing from an English money value at the place of production, upon articles of consumption, the true value of which is their food-sustaining power to the people who consume them." I was invited, therefore, to proclaim myself "conscience-stricken" at this "overwhelming refutation," and was called upon to admit that my inference was "purely nonsensical." But, as I immediately pointed out in reply, I made no such blunder, nor anything at all like it. This will very presently appear, and then perhaps I, too, may ask for a little contrition, I, too, may demand that such misrepresentations should be withdrawn and disavowed.

For how stand the facts? The test was applied to the Punjab, the richest province in all India with the exception of a few districts in Bengal. In such terrible haste, however, was the newly-appointed Famine Commissioner to make the best of his way from the India Office to Printing House Square with his "overwhelming refutation" in his pocket, that he, a professional agriculturist of the highest note, absolutely forgot to make any deduction whatever for seed grain, or to take account of the amount of corn necessary for the cattle, in his calculation of what was available for the sustenance of 17,000,000 human beings in the Punjab.

One would have supposed that, after such astounding oversights as these, a man like Mr. John Morley would have been slow to adopt Sir James Caird's conclusions without further examination, and that Sir Erskine Perry might have told off a few India Office clerks if only to save him from overstating his case. Not so. It is even asserted in the official argument which the former writer has fathered, that bullocks in India do not have feeds of corn, and that "practically hardly any part of the human food-supply goes to the cattle." Will it be believed that this is absolutely erroneous? Would any one imagine, on looking at that assertion, that there is not a single well-kept horse, bullock, milch-cow, camel, or donkey in the Punjab but gets grain when in work? Yet this is undoubtedly the fact. And there are in the Punjab 6,000,000 cattle and horses. In checking Sir James Caird's calculation, therefore, by the light of his own statistics, this important error must be constantly remembered, as the horses and cattle of the Punjab may be neglected in the same way—and in the same way only—as similar animals in England when considering the quantity of food at the disposal of the country.

Sir James Caird said that, after allowance is made for taxation, the native of the Punjab has 2 lbs. of grain a day per head, "which is more than twice the amount consumed per head in England." My friend, Mr. Boyd Kinnear, at once pointed out, in a letter to me, that this was manifestly incorrect, and that Sir James Caird had even omitted to deduct the chaff from the weight of Punjab grain. By Sir James Caird's own figures, too, given in his book on "The Landed Interest and the Supply of Food," the total amount of corn annually consumed in the British Islands is put at 280,000,000 cwts., which, for a population of 33,500,000, would give 2 lbs. 9 ozs. a day, instead of the less than 1 lb. a day used by Sir James for the purpose of controversy. No doubt a deduction must be made for so much of the inferior grains used for the cattle, horses, etc., as in the Punjab, and a portion of the barley which is malted; but, on the other hand, there are 116,000,000 cwts. of potatoes apart from other vegetables, which allow for an additional 17 ozs. of potatoes per head per day. Thus, allowing nothing for the 4½ ozs. of meat and the ounce of cheese and butter, also tabulated by Sir James Caird, the Englishman has for consumption 2 lbs. 9 ozs. of corn and 1 lb. 1 oz. of potatoes a day against the 2 lbs. per head for the Punjabee, much of which consists of very inferior grains. So much for Sir James Caird's statement, adopted and enforced by official authority.

A further examination of his calculation would show that it is untrustworthy from one end to the other. The gaol rate of diet I will not insist upon. Nevertheless, it is above that which the great mass of Punjabee labourers can afford; and none can doubt that even in the Punjab, which may be fairly called the "garden of India," the condition of the mass of the people is not very satisfactory, or that pressure brings them at once within the grip of starvation and famine. That such pressure occurs but rarely is due to the natural fertility of the soil and the abundant supply of water. Nor should it be overlooked that the produce of the country, estimated at the highest rates, shows a miserably small income, though prices are taken on the spot. When 40*s*. or even 50*s*. per head of agricultural produce is apportioned to the supply of the various appurtenances of life, the Punjabee has little overplus left for other purposes when his most ordinary wants are supplied. To say that I have made an error in assuming the common value of the rupee as a basis of calculation is a serious mistake. The absurdity, such as there is, did not rest with me. How dangerous also large exports of food-grains may be even here has been seen recently from the effect produced in the southern districts of this comparatively prosperous province.

But, taking another part of India, what in any other country would be the value of the grain called *kesari*, which is said by the official reports to be very unwholesome, producing loin-palsy, and yet is largely eaten by the peasantry because they can afford nothing else? Surely the most sensational figures scarcely give a fair idea of poverty such as this.

Again, turning to the North-West Provinces, I find that Mr. Morley argued that grain is frequently as dear as 10 lbs. for a shilling without producing any distress. 10 lbs. for a shilling means 10 seers for a rupee. Once more, therefore, I am amazed, as one ignorant of India, at the boldness of this assertion, for I find, on turning to the famine reports for 1876 and 1877, that when wheat—the dearest grain commonly eaten—rose in price from 19 seers to 16 seers for the rupee, that is to say when 16 lbs., not 10 lbs., could be purchased for a shilling, Mr. Edwards, the commissioner, writes of Budaon and other districts of the North-West Provinces: "Prospects very gloomy. Agricultural labourers already in great straits." It was the opinion of many of the district officials that relief works ought to have been started immediately. 10 lbs. for a shilling is a *famine price* in the North-West Provinces, the ordinary average, if properly calculated, being over 25 seers for a rupee, or more than 25 lbs. for a shilling.

It is the more strange that this extraordinary statement should have been made, seeing that an elaborate volume of the "Prices of Food-grains throughout India from 1861-1876" was published in June 1878 at Calcutta. This work is now before me, and in 1875-76 wheat averaged 24 seers for the rupee, or 24 lbs. for the shilling, and great millet (*jowari*) nearly 30 seers for the rupee, or 30 lbs. for the shilling. Not even during the great famines of 1860-61 and 1868-69 did either wheat or millet reach so low an average as 10 lbs. for a shilling!

I leave it to others to determine what such criticism as this is worth. As is now well known, 300,000 or 400,000 people died of starvation in these very provinces, which had been and were then exporting grain to Madras. The average income of the people in a good year has been taken at over 35*s.*; 27*s.* is the value of the agricultural produce alone. But I never pretended that the figures which I adopted were absolutely accurate; I used them merely because I found they were far better than any others that were attainable, and because, as Sir Erskine Perry admitted, the agricultural statistics of India are still shamefully imperfect. It may be said, indeed, that although two costly departments are maintained in England and in India, none of any value are furnished to the public at all. The very criticisms which have been levelled at the calculations I took, lead me to believe that, though necessarily rough in some respects, those figures are much nearer the truth than I could have imagined possible. No one, at any rate,—certainly not Sir James Caird,—has yet pointed out any error in them worthy of note. It is distressing, nevertheless, to see a question of such gravity as this of the impoverishment of India discussed in such a spirit as the above statement as to the price of grain bears witness to on the part of the great officials who furnished Mr. Morley with his data. A very different tone might surely have been expected from the men who are directly to blame for much of what has occurred.

A letter from "T. H. T.," published in a morning paper, traversed my figures with respect to the Punjab. It is not a little remarkable that all the official apologists fasten upon this particular province, and I might fairly point out that in so far as the Punjab has been prosperous, it was in consequence of the very system of light assessment that has been recommended. Even here, however, of late years the plan of raising the land tax and imposing local cesses has been adopted with the usual results. The Punjab is, however, as I have said, the garden of India. "T. H. T." puts the value of the total produce for 17,500,000 people at £41,000,000 for a most favourable year, and makes out that if the whole population were fairly well nourished and lodged, there would be a surplus of £6,000,000 a year. Without going through his calculations at full length, it will perhaps be sufficient if I point out that he, like Sir James Caird, takes scarcely any account of seed, and that even according to his own administration report, he greatly understates the cost of gaol food and clothing, which last year averaged 46*s.* throughout the Punjab. It will be observed that by "T. H. T.'s" own figures, the average income per head is only 47*s.* I do not see, therefore, that on this gentleman's own showing there is such a high standard of prosperity in the Punjab, even when allowance is made for women and children. In any case, the estimates I made applied to the whole of India, and if the North-West Provinces alone were taken, the poverty of the people would be yet more conspicuous.

Once again. It is said with special reference to the North-West Provinces—and Sir John Strachey was long Lieutenant-Governor of those Provinces—that no matter how severe the scarcity, "the agricultural classes are not forced to go to the professional grain-dealers." I am told also, with some asperity, that I altogether misrepresent the facts when I say—and I take leave here to repeat and enforce my remark—that the agriculturists over large tracts "are so miserably destitute that they come upon the Government relief-works at the very commencement of the slightest scarcity." It seems to me a pity that no pains were taken to refer to works so easily accessible as the Famine Reports before point-blank contradictions of this kind are offered to the public on the highest official authority. It seems strange, I say, the statement should be hazarded that these poor people "lived on their own stocks; many profited by the high prices, and very few suffered from them," when I am enabled to oppose a direct official contradiction penned at the time to this allegation.

Thus Mr. C. A. Daniell writes: "In the whole division (Jhansi) the difficulty which presents itself now is this. The poorer class of cultivators, the ploughmen and labourers, cannot get food except with great difficulty. The banias close their advances to the cultivators, and the labourers have no work to do. . . . When the same crop is endangered by drought, the banias close their money-bags, and refuse food or its equivalent." And similar reports are forwarded of other districts. In the North-West Provinces, in fact, the main difficulty was that there were not stores of food to the amount calculated upon, relief-works were not started early enough, and the people died of what was, after all, a moderate scarcity.

But it is urged that the selling price of land in both the Punjab and North-West Provinces has largely increased during the last twenty years, and the Lieutenant-Governors of these two great provinces gave this at Calcutta as irrefragible evidence of the increased prosperity of the people. This by no means follows. In Ireland, under the system of cottier tenancy, precisely the same phenomenon was to be observed. The competition for holdings increased and the prices of the goodwill rose, but the people were getting poorer all the time. This, therefore, by itself, is no proof of growing welfare, and no other than official opinions are given as to the improvement in the appearance of the people. What does not yet seem fully understood is that it rests with a foreign Government, whose subjects are dying so largely of starvation, to *prove* that the foreign rule is in no sense the cause of this terrible state of things. It is no answer to these famine-stricken people to put forward merely *ex cathedra* opinions on their well-being. To say we must spend £19,000,000 on the army to keep the country, to urge that we must remit £20,000,000 worth of agricultural produce to Europe without return for the services we render, sounds but poor reasoning to the miserable cultivator, who is tottering to his death for the want of that very exported food.

"D." seems to have appreciated this in some degree, and devoted himself to showing that the condition of the people *is* improving, in spite of what has been said. One or two instances of his method will suffice. For example, the reassessed districts chosen in Bombay, so far from being "taken at random," are among the most prosperous in the province. To prove how dangerous it is to rely upon this official gentleman's figures, I need only take the table of the increase of cattle in Bombay, p. 790. It is said, and I do not dispute the statement, that the amount of agricultural stock held by the cultivators is, to a certain extent, some test of their prosperity. Beyond all question, if it could be shown that the number of cattle owned by the people in Bombay had increased in numbers without any deterioration in quality, this would be by itself one strong indication of enhanced well-being. "D." gives the number of cows, bullocks, and *buffaloes* at 5,723,066 for 1871-2, and 7,113,376 for 1876-77, thus showing the enormous increase of 1,390,310 in the five years.

But on turning to the Bombay Administration

Reports for these two years, I found to my astonishment that the 5,723,066 given for 1871-72 are the figures for cows and bullocks only, no buffaloes at all being here reckoned, whereas to the total for 1876-77 buffaloes to the number of no fewer than 1,603,900 are added. The figures for 1876-77 are wrong also by 100,000, the correct total being 7,013,376, and not 7,113,376. The true totals for cows and bullocks in Bombay are 5,723,066 for 1871-72 and 5,409,476 for 1876-77. Thus, instead of the *increase* of 1,390,310 claimed for Bombay in the five years, there was a *decrease* in that period of no less than 313,590!

What the result of the famine was I do not stop to inquire, for after this I think I need not check "D.'s" investigations further. I said, however, that bullocks were decreasing in number and going off in quality. I will establish this proposition in another quarter. At p. 22 of the Deccan Riots Report, presented to Parliament last session, is to be found a comparison of the census of 1843 with that for 1873 for 219 villages of the Ahmednuggur Collectorate. What do I read? That during these thirty years the cows decreased by 2,000, and the sheep and goats by 16,000. To those who desire to go deeper into this question, let me recommend the remarks of the late Mr. Carpenter at pp. 69 and 76 of the same Report on the effect of the enhanced assessments. In spite of the great impulse given by the American cotton famine, even Bombay is now again on the downward path.

I have dealt with these mistakes at some length, for they go to the very root of the matter. When the whole official evidence of prosperity thus tumbles to pieces at the first touch of examination, surely Englishmen at home must be satisfied that the affairs of their Indian Empire need the gravest consideration, and that mere official declarations must no longer pass unchallenged and unchecked.

There are times and seasons in the affairs of nations, when responsibility is forced home to those who have neglected, evaded, or abused it—and these that we live in are of them. The process hitherto in favour for the regeneration of India has been tried and found wanting. We have now to retrace our steps, and render our noble dependency a gain and a strength to the whole Empire, by a wider policy, resting upon native growth under European guidance, not upon the mistaken methods of wholesale Europeanisation.

It is this Europeanisation which is, in fact, at the bottom of all the growing impoverishment. We are not only promoting a system of absenteeism on a scale such as has never been seen before, but there has been hitherto an ever-increasing tendency to employ Europeans in India itself. The large European army, to begin with, takes a vast sum from the pockets of the people; but this expenditure, though it might be greatly reduced, cannot be, of course, removed. In the railways, however, and elsewhere, every European employed takes so much from a native, and still further impoverishes the country by his remittances home. Each new machine that is imported has the same effect—that of requiring more European attendants; and the value of these improvements, so far as the people of

India is concerned, is thus heavily handicapped from the outset. What the effect of Irish absenteeism is in aggravating Irish poverty is now a matter of history. The rent of Ireland is remitted in the form of agricultural produce to the absentee landlords, instead of being spent among the people or in improving the estates. Even taking the view that the land-tax of India is also rent, we have the same phenomenon upon an almost inconceivably greater scale. All the pensions, all the remittances, all the payments for the expensive and unnecessary establishments here at home, represent so much deducted from the produce of the soil and the possible capital of India, to maintain foreigners. Instead of training natives for the works of engineering, in which they have always excelled, we maintain a costly establishment to provide yet more young Europeans to deplete the country. There is not even work for them to do—but still the revenues of India are laid under contribution to protect their vested interests. India pays for all, and, being wholly unrepresented, cannot effectively complain. If these salaries were paid to natives, they would keep the money in the country; and the frightful economical drain, which is producing such deadly effects on the people, would be so far stanched.

What an absurdity, then, is it to talk of taxes levied and used in this way as if there were any similarity between a Government of this sort and a native rule, or the rule of foreigners who lived in the country! A native rajah who receives his land-tax in kind, and spends it on the spot in supporting the relatives and friends of those from whom it is taken, can deduct a much larger percentage without harm than a foreign Government, which exacts its tax in money, irrespective of the season, and uses it to pay foreign agency, or to remit to a distant country.* Sir William Sleeman, whose work Sir Erskine Perry quoted with high approval, pointed out all this most forcibly more than forty years ago, and it is at least worthy of consideration that the very men, who, like Sir William, knew most of the natives, and took the largest share in bringing about those reforms which all readily admit to be advantageous, were most bitterly opposed to that unreasoning

* In his despatch of August 8th, 1878, to Sir Henry Layard, Lord Salisbury insists upon the modification of the Turkish system of farming the revenue and a substitution of "the arrangement known in India as a settlement." "The tithe system . . . is condemned by universal experience, and will scarcely find an advocate." By December 4th, 1878, the Turks having pointed out, in the meantime, that such a reform had better be tried in the first instance in a peaceful province, Lord Salisbury had changed his mind on this point. He admits that the introduction of the settlement "would be attended with many difficulties even in the hands of a highly-skilled Administrator; and under the conditions which prevail in Turkey, it must be introduced gradually and with precaution. *If the assessment is fixed too high, or if, in countries subject to failure of crop, it is not modified by a sufficiently elastic system of remission, it may be productive of great misery, and may end in fixing upon the peasantry the rule of the local usurer, which has been found to be more oppressive than even that of the tithe-farmer.*" Whence did Lord Salisbury derive this result of settlement? Beyond all question from India, where our rigid inelastic system has been too often "productive of great misery" and has ended "in fixing upon the peasantry the rule of the local usurer." Surely this admission on the part of the Minister for Foreign Affairs, who had only just quitted the India Office after four years of almost absolute rule, ought to teach a little modesty to some of our Anglo-Indian officials.

Europeanisation of the country which has landed us in our present terrible difficulties. It is useless to argue that a Government is doing well for a people who are suffering, as the natives of India have been suffering, under our rule. Say what we may to the effect that one-third of the total gross exports meeting with no return represents merely interest on capital supplied by England to India in one form or another, India still pays far too dear for her advantages. Granted that English administration is even good in itself, we have here too much of it for the interest both of England and India.

It so happens that there is a direct example of the effect of the two methods—the one of appointing a very few Europeans merely to superintend and improve the native administration, and gradually introduce an improved system suited to the people; the other to pitchfork Europeans into every office of consequence, and force departments and public works upon the country almost without calculation as to their effects. In Mysore the two plans followed one after the other. Sir Mark Cubbon administered that province of 5,000,000 people with four Europeans, at a cost, for the European agency, of £13,000 a year. He used his influence as far as possible to check the abuses and foster the advantages of the native local administrations, encouraged the construction of public works by the natives themselves, insisted on light taxation, and abstained from continuous petty intermeddling. What was the result? In 1861-62, though Mysore had suffered from short monsoons and consequently bad average harvests since 1853, the people were, beyond all question, in a state of the greatest prosperity. Distraint for land-tax had become almost unknown. Notwithstanding all this attention to the welfare of the people, the surplus for the year was £105,000, and there were no less than ninety-six lakhs of rupees, or nearly one million sterling in the treasury. These were, indeed, the golden days of Mysore, and the cultivators were living in comfort, almost in wealth. There were drawbacks of course, but they were small compared with the benefits; and to this day the people look back with bitter regret to the happiness they experienced under that light and considerate rule.

But soon after this the new methods were commenced in full force. The European agency cost £90,000 a year instead of £13,000; public works were pressed on with vigour; the *rêgime* of desk-work and bureau administration was the order of the day; the surplus disappeared, and the reserve in the chest was soon drawn out. Mysore, which, under Sir Mark Cubbon's gentle sway, had been the most prosperous foreign state under our control, went steadily from bad to worse. The condition of the cultivators became deplorable; the soil deteriorated, so that, as Mr. Harman's report shows, the matter has become one of the gravest consequence; and then a drought swept away so large a proportion of the population that positively the officials, whose well-meant earnestness contributed so largely to the catastrophe, failed in their efforts to number the dead.

All this has taken place within a few years, and under the very eyes of men now in England, whose evidence the Government can obtain and verify with little trouble. It is not that European administration is necessarily ruinous. That we can see from the admirable result of Sir Mark Cubbon's careful administration. It is not that public works are not highly beneficial. These, when judiciously made out of savings, enhance, and ever must enhance, the well-being of a lightly-taxed population. But when European agency and public works are alike overdone; when foreign salaries and foreign systems are imposed upon the population to an extent which savours of the very fanaticism of so-called improvement,—then, as we see, the result is starvation, ruin, and death—a famine-stricken people and an exhausted soil.

Lord Cranbrook's despatch of November 7th, 1878, in answer to Lord Lytton, showed an inclination to remedy this great evil. But, as the then Secretary of State for India himself pointed out, his predecessors for years past have insisted as strongly as himself upon the employment of natives in the Government service, and yet very little has been done in this way. I fear that, until a law is passed to the effect that only certain great superior offices shall be held by Europeans, and that all other appointments, covenanted and uncovenanted, the berths now held by Englishmen in railways, engineering works, and, in short, in every department, shall be filled up by qualified natives as the present holders drop off and leave the country—until this is done, no permanent good will be wrought. The influence of the Government should be exerted for the future, not as heretofore to find additional employment for Europeans, and thus intensify the fatal drain from the resources of India; but to raise the native administrators to the same level as that of the native judges, of whose capacity all speak so highly, while insuring that a genuine control is exerted by Englishmen not overburdened with that excessive office-work that now removes them farther and farther from the mass of the people. To develop native talent, to encourage native originality in every department, is surely a nobler aim than to depress a whole community, comprising one-sixth of the human race, by a superincumbent mass of foreigners, who live less and less in the country, and therefore know less and less of it.

One of the saddest results of our present action is the decay of native arts and manufactures. According to the testimony of officials who have devoted especial attention to this matter, the impoverishment of the country, and the reduction of the native population to one dead level of poverty-stricken agriculturists, are utterly crushing out the beautiful native art-work in our territories. The statements in Dr. Birdwood's "Handbook for the Indian Court at Paris" show what a mischievous effect the cheap gaol-work, brought into competition with the manufactures of honest artisans, has produced upon more than one important industry.

I am told, however, by my official critics that India is lightly taxed. They are bold men to say it. A bureaucracy acting almost unchecked by European, and wholly unchecked by native opinion, can hazard observations with impunity in India, that read strangely when put side by side with other official observations in England. Here is an instance. Madras is lightly taxed, so lightly that Sir John Strachey has found it convenient to raise the salt-tax in that province, in a famine year, over forty per cent. Now listen to the Government of Madras itself, speaking about the people under its rule :—

"*The Madras ryot is very heavily taxed;* five rupees for wet (single crop) and one rupee for dry being his average assessment. . . . Let the extent and nature of their holdings be considered. The number of leases is 2,392,064; of these 38,825 only are above 100 rupees, while upwards of one million and a quarter are below ten rupees. The average extent of a holding is eight acres, and the average assessment payable is fifteen rupees or thirty shillings sterling. How are two million peasant proprietors of this kind to pay sixty shillings apiece next year, after a season of unprecedented calamity, which, in addition to other sufferings and losses, has brought about already the destruction of a great portion of their cattle, and will cause the loss of many more?"

How indeed? But we shall take order with them somehow, we may depend upon it, and the extra forty per cent. on salt will still further improve their position. But, I ask, what sort of administration is this which, in the face of Dr. Cornish's official declaration that the poor ryots and agricultural labourers could not even before afford enough salt to keep themselves and their cattle in health, indulges in such terrible irony as to demand "arrears of revenue," and claps a prohibitive duty on a necessary of life?

I pass on. I asked, Where is the wealth of India?

Not one yet has told us. Its poverty is conspicuous enough. Even the most sanguine of Anglo-Indians admit that no more taxation can be raised with safety; and if there are those great accumulations what is being done with them? They are hoarded, it is said; the people will not either lend or invest. Surely this seems almost incredible among a population where interest-charges for advances is a subject thoroughly understood by every class of the community, and recovery of debt under our system is only too easy. All the gold and silver imported into India from the beginning of this century up to 1878 amounts to only £382,000,000, which is but £2 per head of population after all, and is assuredly no excessive supply of the precious metals for a country which rests now upon a silver currency, and where £50,000,000 of revenue is yearly collected in that metal. The import of bullion is at any rate far more than compensated by the drain from new resources already insisted upon.

It is the constant lamentation that neither capitalists nor agriculturists develop the country. Yet it has been noted on all hands that the agricultural class in particular, the moment they are able to scrape a few rupees together, and have a full security of tenure, set to work to improve their property. During the period of the one great windfall India has had—the American Civil War—the improvements made by the people of Bombay in their houses and the way of life were most marked. Moreover, as showing how beneficial their prosperity would be to England, a brisk demand for all articles of small luxury sprang up at once. The very agricultural labourers also, who drag on a miserable existence in India, when transported as coolies to Trinidad and British Guiana, speedily save money, and in many instances become well-to-do people. The impression that they are bad and wasteful cultivators is one which dies away, I find, in proportion to the amount of attention the observer has devoted to the matter. They cannot save, cannot accumulate, cannot improve, because the taxation, and the way in which the taxation is levied and spent, ruin them.

There is not a country in the world which, after twenty years of peaceful, orderly, and well-intentioned rule, could present so little to show for it in the way of increased well-being as India in 1878. Its total sea-borne trade, even including that which is carried on between the Indian ports, was utterly insignificant for so vast a population, although £150,000,000 at least had been spent in improving communications during those twenty years. What is needed, therefore, are not mere dictatorial opinions by high-placed officials as to the wealth and contentment of the provinces which they administer, but undoubted facts which shall outweigh the terrible evidence of increasing famine to the contrary. At present no such facts are forthcoming.

I now come once more to the question of the public works. It is at least remarkable that Mr. John Morley, who must be looked upon as the principal official champion, does not touch my argument on this head at all. I may take it for granted, therefore, that up to the present time the public works, especially the railways, have represented a dead pecuniary loss to the country. Now no doubt the guaranteed lines are beginning to look as if a profit might shortly be expected in an ordinary year; but when the loss by exchange is calculated, this is not even yet the case. As to the State lines, the position is far worse; for, as I showed in the last chapter, the £17,000,000 expended on them up to 1879 did not show a return of even 1 per cent. upon the capital. Taking the interest of the money at only 4 per cent., the natives of India were forced to lose £500,000 a year on this single investment. But this might have been anticipated. The original trunk lines connecting the great cities and centres of commerce, although built in the most extravagant way possible, and at a preposterous cost, might be expected to pay 5 per cent. in time, if only by the mere export trade; but these new lines are hopeless affairs in the majority of instances, and the prospect of a profitable return is remote indeed.

Notwithstanding all this, Sir John Strachey imposed additional taxation to the amount of £1,500,000 mainly upon the poorest class of the people, for the express purpose of creating a "famine insurance fund." This very £1,500,000 so levied from the famine-stricken inhabitants of Madras, Bombay, and the North-West Provinces, is expended, not in providing against future famines, as the name would imply, but in extending those unprofitable railways and irrigation works, which are already so heavy a burden on the population.* Mr. Morley did not

* "I am convinced that the imposition of any large amount of fresh taxation in India is impossible without serious practical risk."—Sir John Strachey, February 6th, 1874.

deny this. But can any human being, then, understand what is meant by the statement he so charitably fathered? Instead of borrowing £1,500,000 to spend on "productive" works, which all previous experience has shown prove unproductive nine times out of ten, the finance minister imposes heavy taxation in a famine year, to apply to this same purpose, and then claims credit for extinguishing yearly an equal amount of the debt.

Verily we have here a scheme for the Insurance of Famine, if ever one was set afoot. We drag food from half-starved people to build these State railways, and then wonder that starvation is perpetuated by the process. Lord Lytton proclaimed that £10,000,000, ought to be spent in similar fashion in the North-West Provinces. I rejoice to believe that these hare-brained schemes are now meeting with a check, and that this terrible mania for public works, which yearly absorbs £6,000,000, £7,000,000, £8,000,000 of the revenue, may shortly receive its quietus.*

I must deal briefly with a few more of Mr. Morley's remarks. (1) In touching on the local and municipal cesses, the writer challenges my figures, but gives none of his own to correct them by. (2) The Sikh Government, whatever its drawbacks, levied *one-tenth* of the salt-tax we get out of the Punjab. (3) Mr. Morley says that I am guilty of "a singular inconsistency," because I extol a light permanent settlement as "one of my panaceas," and in the next breath deplore "the miserable, abject condition of the Bengal ryot."

* In this I was deceived, as will hereafter appear.

Mr. Morley himself can never have written this. "The miserable, abject condition of the Bengal ryot" is not my remark at all, as Mr. Morley would have seen had he referred back to my statement. I am in favour of a light permanent settlement undoubtedly, and though that of Bengal was made by Lord Cornwallis with the wrong people, it has been a great boon to the Province. (4) If Mr. Morley will examine into the facts he will find that in many districts the ryots who had got out of the hands of the money-lenders have been thrown back into them by the rigidity of our assessment. (5) How is it, if the North-West Provinces are so much improved as Mr. Colvin alleges, wages, according to the "Moral and Material Progress" for 1872-3, "have scarcely varied at all since the early part of this century, and after payment of the rent the margin left for the cultivator's subsistence is less than the value of the labour expended on the land"? (6) Indian investments are, as I said, almost unknown; and Mr. John Morley himself shows what a ridiculously small fraction of the total debt is held in India. What is more, it has decreased of late years. (7) The import of cotton has ruined the weavers. When the employment of a whole caste is destroyed, and they are reduced to pauperism, I can see, free-trader though I am, that more harm is done than all the free-trade maxims will salve over in India in one generation. (8) I put the home charges since 1857 at £270,000,000 at least. But, says Mr. Morley, "a large amount is, for example, interest on capital which has been most profitably invested in railways." The total amount so paid since 1857-58 is £28,000,000, excluding net traffic receipts; or including these about one-fifth of the total, £270,000,000. Besides the profitable investment is a matter itself in dispute. But when I read Mr. Morley's concluding sentences, his "most sombre views," his certainty that there is "boundless room for improvement in all our methods," I wonder what possessed him to come forward to champion, in this half-hearted way, the system which evidently he sees the weakness of as clearly as I do.

Meanwhile, however, the mischievous policy goes relentlessly on, and endless misery is engendered because Indian financiers will not see that to force natives to borrow at 12 to 60 per cent., to pay taxes which are invested to lose 3 per cent., is as baneful a superstition as ever blighted the fortunes of a people. For this is what it means. Every rupee thus foolishly squandered, every anna thus wantonly taken from the pockets of the people, is another step towards the hopeless impoverishment of the whole country.

Until we can build public works out of savings from a really light taxation, until we have stanched, in part at least, this exhausting economical drain, every public work—no matter how promising to start with—should be charged as unremunerative, and no further mock surpluses should be foisted on Parliament. For they are mock surpluses still. The deficits of the three years 1876, 1877, 1878 have been, as I stated, over £16,000,000, and it is futile for the Indian Government to deny its own figures, or to claim works as "productive" on which, by their own showing, they lose not less than 3 per cent.

So obvious is the peril of the situation, that all sorts of schemes are floating about to relieve debt by counting two and two as five. But there is no financial philosopher's stone to transmute the famine and deficits of extravagance and miscalculation into prosperity and surplus. The total net revenue of India, even now that the extra taxation has been imposed, is scarcely £40,000,000 a year, and of this sum little short of one-half will be expended in home charges alone, when the loss by exchange is taken into account. Apart from the gradual substitution of natives for Europeans in all branches of administration and management, which, though absolutely necessary, must be in its nature a slow process, the only hope of improvement lies in persistent economy, in a relentless determination to curtail home expenditure, and in the encouragement of those simple native methods of agricultural development, which have been so ruinously neglected to foster more ambitious but less beneficial projects. Only now are we beginning to understand that forests, groves, tanks, and wells do more to enrich a poor tropical country than vast systems of railroads and irrigation works.

Economy must commence with the army, the public works, and the home expenditure. In these departments alone at least £6,000,000 a year might be saved to the positive gain of both England and India. It is needless, however, to point out what grave difficulties will be encountered. There will be plenty to cry out at every turn that the "services" are being ruined, because the country is being benefited at the expense of the lifelong prejudices of an official class. But first let these show that they are in any way entitled to a hearing, for they, and their whole administration, are on their trial. What have they done? The results of this excessive Europeanisation, and of this Pelion upon Ossa of paper government, we see. It has crushed the very life out of the people we rule. Surely it is high time to try less heroic methods. Every thousand pounds drawn away from India unnecessarily to pay expensive European agency, pensions, and interest, on unremunerative public works, is so much capital diverted from profitable investment in our dependency—so much taken from profitable purchases to be made from our own people. Impoverishment in India means stagnation in England and distress in our own manufacturing centres. When the interests alike of England and of India are on one hand, and the mistaken theories of a bureaucracy on the other, who can doubt which will have to stand aside?

It is on this ground that appeal may be fearlessly made to see that the well-being of our fellow-subjects is far more to our advantage than a steady decline in their prosperity, owing to a system which benefits but few among us. If we cannot keep India save by inflicting perpetual impoverishment and starvation upon an increasing number of the population, then we cannot leave the country too soon. It was no economical bigot who proclaimed that India could be defended and governed for £30,000,000 a year, and that every rupee sent in addition did but work injury to the population; it was no mere sciolist who contended that the cost of the army ought never to exceed £12,500,000. All admit the extravagance, but no one has yet shown the courage and determination to apply the necessary remedies. To say that in future India must be governed for the sake of its inhabitants, means undoubtedly the displacement in the future of most of our own countrymen from offices in that country. But we cannot shrink from this necessary change because of its difficulty or the opposition it wil provoke. As years pass on, our constant endeavour must be to secure our position by the welfare, prosperity, and, as far as possible, the self-government of the immense population under our control. The work may be troublesome, but the end is noble, and the reward is sure. Planting a great policy is like planting a great tree; we may never live to see it in full vigour, but generations to come shall bless us for its beauty and its shade.

III.

BLEEDING TO DEATH.

THE economical condition of our Indian Empire is in itself, unfortunately, no very attractive subject. We need, it seems, a continuous succession of "sensational" events to keep the minds of Englishmen fixed upon a subject where we all incur day by day the heaviest responsibility. For the good government and improvement of India form the duty and concern not of officials alone, but of every man who can see wherein lies the true greatness of an empire. To raise the people of India to a higher level by steady help given to their better native customs, to increase their wealth by reducing the cost of administration, and a cautious suggestion of improvements in their agriculture and their industries—to educate them in the widest sense, so that in due time they may be able to administer their own country—these are aims and objects which surely claim from us more than the fitful attention which they at present receive—ought rather to rouse the energies and quicken the imagination of all. We have no right to look at the bright side of what has been done, and shut our eyes to the stupendous dangers ahead of us.

Dr. W. W. Hunter not long since recounted what

has been done by our efforts—efforts well paid for by the people—and not the most disaffected native could deny that in perfect religious liberty, peace, and protection, the suppression of organised gangs of robbers and stranglers, the safety of women, the freedom of internal trade, the security of lands and goods, and in some districts the improvement of communication, we have conferred great benefits upon India. These are results of our rule which we may well look upon with satisfaction, and may reasonably hope will long produce a good effect. But, with the single exception of the last, they were each and all carried out by the East India Company, and are due to the men of the last generation. Let them, then, be credited with these good deeds, not the men of to-day. Our present officials work with equal zeal and equal earnestness,—I do not dispute it for a moment,—but they do so over a great part of India under conditions in which it is impossible that they should succeed. The perfection of our civil administration, the exquisite beauty of our system of minute-writing and elaborate checks, even the unquestionable uprightness of the whole official class, carry but cold comfort to a starving people.

That famines are becoming more frequent and more fatal, that taxation has reached its limit, that the revenue is inelastic and the expenditure period for period steadily increasing; that the production of the soil over large areas is lessening, and the margin of food above the limit of starvation being greatly reduced, are hard facts no longer to be put contemptuously aside as the idle fancies of so-called pessimists—they are the well-weighed conclusions of a Special Famine Commissioner convinced against his will, the accepted truths of the English Government which felt but now assured that India was rejoicing in the fullest prosperity. It is no light work to right past mistakes, or to treat with justice and generosity a people wholly dependent upon us for their welfare and their safety. The mischiefs of over-Europeanisation and economical error are far-reaching in their effects—the remedies can be but gradually applied. But do not let us deceive ourselves: the next great famine, unless persistent care is taken, will be something unprecedented in history, and no mere temporary expedients will ward off the danger.

Under our direct rule in India we have no fewer than two hundred millions of people, and there are besides fifty millions more in native states who are indirectly controlled by us. Yet all this vast mass of human beings is kept in order by an army of 60,000 Europeans and 120,000 natives, exclusive of the native police. It is impossible to put the naturally peaceful character of the people in a more striking way. There have probably never been more than 300,000 Europeans in the country at any one time; and yet since we have been in possession the only serious rising has been that of our own troops. Notwithstanding, too, the death by starvation of millions, there has been no really dangerous outbreak among the numerous races we govern. Any other society would have broken up under such a strain as that to which some districts in India were exposed. But the fierce fighting men of the northwest have so far been as patient in trial as the milder populations of Madras and Bengal. This says much for them, and much also for their belief that in spite of many drawbacks we mean to rule honestly and well.

The fate of the Dacoity leader, Wassadeo Bulwunt Phadke, afforded clear evidence that the population is now, as ever, ready to side with authority, even where they think themselves oppressed, otherwise he had everything in his favour.* The Deccan has suffered much from usurers and from famine. Wassadeo's bold raids appealed to the old Mahratta pedatory instinct. He and his followers might at least enable the hopelessly involved to recover their ancestral lands, of which they consider they have been unjustly deprived. Nevertheless, they showed but little sympathy with the marauders; the leader was consequently captured and his band dispersed. In spite of grievous mismanagement, the Rumpa disturbances in Madras, brought about likewise by our own neglect, died down without any assistance from the outside. Still, therefore, the often-repeated remark remains true, that so long as the agricultural classes are well affected we shall have no great difficulty in keeping our hold upon the country. It is an absolute necessity, therefore, to take the very best view, that any germs of serious discontent should be taken account of and fairly dealt with.

In the Deccan this is, to a certain extent, being done, and none too soon. After four years of inattention the report of the commission with reference to the outrages upon the money-lenders at last pro-

* This rising was far more popular and more serious than was admitted at the time.

duced an effect, and the bill brought forward by Mr. Hope passed the legislative council. This was by far the most remarkable measure introduced for many years. For it amounted to a distinct confession that our civil courts have proved a complete failure, and have been seriously harmful to the people. What is the remedy? More Europeanisation? Further attempts to force on the country a system for which it is wholly unfit? Not at all. The new measure recognised that we must take a step back, must have less of law and more of justice, must leave the natives to manage their own business, and even endeavour to build up again that which before we have derided and pulled down. When native panchayats are to be re-established and the usurers dealt with on the old native principles, it is clear that we have taken a new view of our duties in India.

A short survey of the Deccan Agriculturists Relief Act will show that in its desire to protect the ryot the Indian Government has gone very near to hamper the ordinary operations of borrower and lender. This may be a fault on the right side, and in so far as it is a return to the native system will probably be worked well by the people themselves; but the entire Act is obviously drawn with the intention of ousting the soucars altogether. The judge is, in fact, given powers which entirely upset the very first principles of freedom of contract, and it is difficult to see what security is left to the money-lender at all unless the custom of the country discountenances breach of agreement. Whilst, therefore, the endeavours to bring cheap justice to the ryot, to give him power to demand accounts at all times, to put a proper system of registration at his disposal, to revert to the old Hindoo law that not more than twice the amount advanced could be demanded of the borrower, and the relief of the agriculturist from liability to imprisonment for debt, are all most salutary reforms, and cannot fail to benefit the district, it is by no means so clear that the other portions of the bill will not deprive the ryot of the chance of borrowing at all. But the important matter is that the Government have entered upon the path of reform.

There is still much to be done even in the Deccan. In the now famous report on this portion of the Bombay Presidency it was distinctly stated that one great cause of the poverty of the ryots,—a poverty which has since resulted in their death by thousands,—in addition to a bad soil, a very variable climate, and the oppression of the money-lenders, was the rigidity with which the revenue was collected, and in some districts the excessive enhancement of the assessment. To this may now be added the pressure for arrears. The rigidity of our exaction of the land revenue is in itself a matter of most serious moment, because it may happen that in a bad year its prompt demand may ruin the ryot or drive him into the hands of those very money-lenders from whom we wish to protect him. Not until this, the very basis of our whole system of rule and taxation, is satisfactorily dealt with, and the home drain staunched, will there be any marked change for the better in the condition of the agriculturists.

Elsewhere also our civil courts are doing mischief,

and over-assessment is crushing the landowners. Similarly reforms are needed in the North-West Provinces and in Oude, in the Punjab, in the Central Provinces, and in Madras. For the same unregarded truths which have been told by some of the district officers for years past have now been confirmed by Sir James Caird from personal observation. He said that it is impossible to view the condition of India without grave apprehension, because owing to various causes the landless class is increasing, whilst there is no greater demand for labour, and—most blighting fact of all—the fertility of the soil is being steadily injured. Here, then, in the opinion of a sound unimaginative Scotchman, who went out to India strongly of the other way of thinking, are all the elements of an appalling economical catastrophe.

Sir Richard Temple pointed out some years ago how the blackguardism of the population seemed, in some to him inexplicable way, to increase under the shadow of our rule. That is to say, both observers, the Englishman fresh from this country, and the Anglo-Indian of thirty years' experience, are agreed that those who do not own land are increasing, whilst there is no occupation to which they can profitably turn. In the North-West Provinces—I am quoting from a Bengal civilian in active employment—the jails are filled with ejected landowners and their dependants. Such is the feeling against the existing system that they would prefer the murder and anarchy of the old native rulers to the hopeless ruin to which they are now exposed. "A land-tax assessed and collected as ours too often is, is not a tax upon income but a tax upon capital." How then can the landowner or small proprietor, how can the mere labourer, who is dependent upon him, keep his head above water? He cannot. It is impossible. He is always coming to that deep part of the stream which the poor ryot spoke of, always finding that to keep himself and his family from starvation he must get further and further into debt, until at last there comes a period of scarcity, and he perishes.

To obviate the admitted drawbacks of our system, a plan has been proposed which already works fairly well in some districts. This is to spread the payment of the land-tax over a period of twenty years, allowing interest at a low rate it paid in advance, and charging it if carried over. But, as the native journals urge, the scheme still makes no due allowance for total remission in years of famine. Here, again, we must return to native methods. Oude, for instance, infamously misgoverned as it was in one sense under the king prior to annexation, was richer, the people were better off, the whole province more valuable than is the case to-day. Sir William Sleeman foresaw this, and protested against the way in which annexation was carried out. A greater blunder, as we can now see, was never made. Politically it was one of the chief causes of the mutiny; financially and economically, it has been a miserable failure. For here, as elsewhere, we have attempted to make a clean sweep of the whole social system, and tried to a great extent that plan of leaving no class between the pauper ryot and the collector, which has had such serious results in other parts of India.

Let us understand, once for all, that apart from the economical mischief done in India during the last twenty years, one civilisation, trying to act upon and improve another, ought to be exceedingly cautious in what it either removes or introduces. For these simple native customs, these quiet never-ending native arrangements, which in too many instances have been swept away, are the growth of thousands of years—what, after all, is a hundred years in the history of a people like this?—and to suppose for a moment that a handful of foreigners, who do not even live in the country, can safely introduce their ideas and methods, irrespective of the opinions of their subjects, is merely to insure that miserable condition which all non-official observers deplore. We have tried two distinct systems of government in India—the one invariably successful, the other a lamentable failure. Yet both secure us supreme control, and enable us to keep in our hands the trade of the country.

Take the case of Baroda. Baroda had a bad native ruler, who was deposed under well-known circumstances. Instead of pursuing the course which was adopted with Oude, or even the principle applied in Mysore, a man trained by ourselves, who had previously reorganised Travancore, and was then usefully employed at Indore—Sir Madhava Rao—was appointed Dewan, and became in effect master of the state, subject only to the light control of the resident. The drawbacks to what has been called Dewanism are manifold, and there is no perfection certainly in the rule of Sir Madhava Rao. But Baroda is flourishing marvellously, the people are well off, and famine is provided against.

Here is an important passage by the resident bearing upon the question of famine. The rainfall in 1878 was from a half to one-third of that of an average year, and the rain did not fall till September—let any one just think what the effect of this would have been in many portions of our own territory—the harvest was accordingly deficient, and the country having been denuded of its old stocks of food grains by export for the Deccan and Madras, prices rose enormously. But there was no famine in Baroda: there was only scarcity. When the rain seemed likely to fail altogether, measures were taken for facing the worst without trouble or fuss.

But what was the financial position of Baroda when this calamity threatened? There was a cash balance to the amount of nearly £670,000 in the treasury, and a reserve of over £1,000,000 in 4 per cent. British Government promissory notes, or £1,670,000 in all. Though, too, the revenue fell off by £130,000 owing to the bad season, and the expenditure increased by nearly £150,000, making a difference of £280,000, on a total income of between £1,300,000 and £1,400,000 (and the Dewan for his own ends is far too liberal to the Palace), the deficit for the year was only £20,000. Nor is this result obtained at the cost of any scamping in the administration; and the army is kept up on a most costly scale. The Courts of Justice are good, and suited to the people. Public works, where they are likely to be really valuable, are built out of savings.

Even so, some say there is too much of European methods, successful as the administration is.

Now all this surely redounds to our credit every bit as much as if Baroda were an integral part of our own territory. It is true hardly any Europeans are employed in the State, but the country is under our control, and Sir Madhava Rao is as much our man as if he had come out to India a competition wallah. And what is going on in Baroda is a direct result of our presence in India. Yet we hear there of no terrible impoverishment, no unjust expulsion of landlords, no bitter outcry against the money-lenders. Improved native methods satisfy the people, fill the exchequer, and there is no constant unendurable drain from the country for European pensions and home charges.

Wherever a similar man has been supported in like manner, a similar result has been obtained. Of Mysore under Sir Mark Cubbon I have already spoken; of Jeypore, much to the same effect might be said. The independent Principality of Bhaunagar was for eight years, 1870-78, under the joint administration of Mr. Percival, a Bombay civilian, and the old State Minister. During this period a complete change took place. The government was reformed in every part, a revenue survey was introduced, and the revenue and trade greatly increased—buildings of all sorts, public offices, schools, hospitals, tanks, roads, bridges, lighthouses. So the Bhaunagar State is now by far the most flourishing in Kattywar, and the cause of its recent and rapid advance is by common consent allowed to have been the benign influence of Mr. Percival's presence. He was the

Mark Cubbon of Kattywar. Notwithstanding a lavish outlay on improvements, there was a large balance, little less than six lakhs, in the treasury when the young Raja came of age. The influence of one European acting with and through natives did all this. My attention has been called to this case of Bhaunagar by Mr. Chester Macnaghten, the Principal of the Rajkumar College at Rajkote Kattywar, an intimate friend of twenty-five years' standing. In a recent private letter to me, he says:—

"The fact is, that under existing circumstances a native state administered under British supervision is almost an ideal of prosperity. This remark is a general one, applying to Travancore, Mysore, etc., as well as to Baroda. While the people are governed in their own simple way, the revenue is not wasted. The peace and prosperity which characterises the rural population of India are maintained, while the corruption and dishonesty which characterise native courts are checked. The system is an inexpensive one to the states which enjoy it, and contains all that is best in British and native methods. I believe it is only true to assert that there is not a single native state in India which, if so administered, will not show a surplus."

How is it, then, I ask, that having tried two methods in India, we stick to the failure—wholesale Europeanisation—and discard the success—native administration under light English control? There is, there can be, but one answer. The vast bureaucratic machine we have created in India is too powerful to be brought under restraint. Able, upright men, who have spent their lives on a work which is breaking in their hands, will not admit—I for one can scarcely blame them—that they have laboured for nought, that the hardest task of the next twenty-five years will be to repair the mischief which they have unwittingly done, which they have done rather with the fullest determination to benefit the country. But whilst we are arguing the people are starving, and the appeal now lies not to Viceroy or Finance Minister, not to Secretary of State or to Parliament, but to the great mass of English people from the Queen downwards. Let them hear, let them determine, let them judge. Will they stand by and see their great dependency sink into bankruptcy, starvation, and ruin—will they cry in rude earnest "Perish India!" rather than override the prejudices of a most pertinacious bureaucracy?

I have been at some pains to obtain a direct comparison by a native between British and native rule, and one has been obtained for me from a source beyond suspicion of favouring the native view. The writer was brought up under us in India, and cultivates land in our territory as well as in native territory. The reasons which he gives for the superior prosperity of the people in the latter are well worth the consideration of the Home Government.

1. The tax on fallow and cultivated land in British territory is the same. In native States fallow is taxed only one-eighth of cultivated land. The result in our territory is that the land is getting rapidly exhausted from want of rest; that the tax raises the price of fodder to such an extent as to render it

profitless to the farmers to breed cattle—so much so that the bullocks are deteriorating.*

2. In native States most grazing land is allowed free of charge; we sell it.

3. Native Government waste land is used as common for depasturing cattle; nothing, or a nominal sum, is charged. We let it by auction.

4. Wells sunk by British ryots on their own lands and at their own expense are charged twelve rupees a year. This is not only manifestly unjust, but acts as a check on improvement.

5. There are none of those local cesses under native rule which work great hardship in British territory.

6. Considerable remissions are made for total and partial failure of crops. In Bombay the revenue was allowed to stand over for only *one* year when the famine was devastating the Deccan.

7. Arrears are frequently allowed to stand over for two or three years, or totally remitted. No interest is charged. We charge heavy interest and allow little time. Recently still harsher regulations have been made.

8. The number of instalments under old native rule was four; we make it two.

9. The expenses of the civil courts, a prolific source of ruin to many a ryot under our rule, the intricate varieties of stamps, "with whose confounding nomenclature I am not conversant," and im-

* The truth is both men and bullocks are deteriorating in our territory all over India. Even our Sikhs are not the men of Chilianwallah. In the native States, owing to better feeding, they retain their vigour.

prisonment for debt, to which the ryot is not liable in native States, make up the chief causes of complaint.

There are others, and these may seem—though to me I confess they do not—individually trifling; but the result in the aggregate is really startling. "The prosperity of a rural community is most satisfactorily estimated from the condition of their farms, the quantity of grain stored up in the house, and the extent of indebtedness. The last is the surest sign of comparison where all other conditions are similar. Now this question of the extent of indebtedness is a test which may very well be applied, as it is practical and easily proved. Yet, according to this observer, the result is against us.

It is found that in villages belonging to a State under our indirect control the total percentage of indebtedness is scarcely above that of the most prosperous ryots living side by side in British territory. The latter consider that a good year in which they get nearly enough to eat after the taxes are paid. Here, then, a distinct comparison is possible. The above statements, I repeat, may be relied upon as at any rate expressing the deliberate opinion of an educated cultivator who was induced to record his views with much diffidence and distrust. His statements unfortunately agree with those from official sources.

Read, for example, Mr, Robertson's paper on "Agriculture in Madras," delivered before the Society of Arts. What do we find, always bearing in mind that Mr. Robertson speaks with official authority? This: that whilst the land is inadequately manured and the breed of the cattle deteriorating; whilst a process of desiccation is going on owing to the removal of forests and jungle; whilst we make no advance in agriculture and encourage no beneficial change—whilst all this deterioration and stagnation is steadily observed, there is over all a system of exacting the revenue the most costly known, and one, besides, which directly discourages improvement in every direction. Yet the proportion of exhausting crops is enormous and increasing. Can we wonder that, all this being so, the productive powers of the soil are calculated to have decreased thirty per cent. at least in thirty years?

Here, then, we see the catastrophe which was laughed at as the alarmism of the ignorant once more directly foreshadowed by the evidence of an expert. But I say again that Bombay and Madras are no exceptional cases, that the same phenomena are to be observed throughout our territory. In the North-West Provinces likewise the land does not, as of old, give forth its abundance, and in Oude, the Punjab, and the Central Provinces we are steadily working up to the same result. And yet we are still content to discuss.

The present higher administration of India is entirely European. There are those who vigorously contend that this is in the eternal fitness of things; that to alter or modify it gravely in any way would be ruinous, to point out its infinite deficiencies is little short of unpatriotic. The trifling promise of improvement already made is even objected to, though for years we have been pledged to employ more natives in every department. But the drawbacks to the present arrangement can never be too frequently urged until a distinct and final change is brought about.

Unlike former conquerors of India we do not live in the country, and, as a consequence, we take out of it each year more than the people can afford. The total net revenue of India is under £40,000,000 a year. Not less than £20,000,000 worth of agricultural produce—more than the entire net income derived by the Government from the land revenue —is sent out of India every year without any direct commercial equivalent. Just think what this (and it is an underestimate by over fifty per cent.) really means.* It means that year after year, in dearth and in plenty, in drought and in flood, £20,000,000 is taken from perhaps the poorest people on the earth to bring to us here in England (or to invest in unremunerative public works); it means that so many millions more are condemned to starvation at the next scarcity; it means that during the twenty years 1858-78 £400,000,000 have been so applied. Call this payment for good administration, gloss it over in any way you please, need we look further for the cause of the growing impoverishment of India? Not a single Englishman would say so if last year, not to speak of years before, £67,000,000, the agricultural rent of the country, had been sent hence to the Continent for nothing. Yet £67,000,000 to England is literally a fleabite compared with what £20,000,000 is to India.

But the worst is to come. The interest, the

* I make no excuse for this frequent repetition. Here is *the* crux of the whole question.

pensions, the home charges which go to make up this amount have hitherto, in great part, been met by the proceeds of loans contracted here for other purposes. But further borrowing simply intensifies the drain, and is at last seen to be ruinous. *In future, consequently, there will be little or no set off.* Is it not, then, the business of every man to attempt to stop this open artery which is draining away the life blood of our great dependency? For let us never forget that all this produce is sent away without any reference whatever to the will of the people of India themselves. Quite apart, therefore, from any question of abstract justice to a subject race, it is of the last importance that only so many Englishmen should be employed in India as are absolutely needed for purposes of security and supervision of natives, and that we should not pay ourselves, out of Indian penury, interest which has never been earned, and pensions in excess of what is needful. For the one great need of India is capital, and that capital we now drain away.

We absolutely refuse, however, to make use of the highest native talent even to serve ourselves in a position where it could not fail to be useful. The ablest finance minister India has ever yet seen was a Hindoo, and he was employed by a Mahommedan emperor whose grandfather conquered India. If we cannot rise to the magnanimity of an Akbar, we ought at least to use in some way the greatest financial capacity the country affords. Hindoos understand accounts just as well as ourselves; they are naturally saving, and beyond all question they know where their countrymen feel the pinch of taxation better than we do. Let us therefore take advantage of their knowledge for our own sakes. But hitherto it has been useless to urge this.*

What Englishmen formerly did in India is, as I have said, open to all. None can forget, or would if they could, the glorious work done by Outram among the Bheels, by Edwardes on the Indus border, by the Lawrences, by Mountstuart Elphinstone, by Sleeman, by Meadows Taylor, by Metcalfe and Malcolm, by Shore, Monro, and Macleod. But these great men worked through native channels; they raised the people under their control by personal intercourse, by endeavouring to understand and enter into native ideas, native fears, hopes, ambitions, even amusements. The time for all this in our own territory seems almost to have gone by. Circumstances have entirely changed. The young men who go out to India no longer look upon the country as their home, no longer are able to get so near to the people as their predecessors. They go out at a later age, theoretically far better acquainted with the people they have to govern—and it would not be difficult to name individual competition wallahs who have distinguished themselves by personal self-sacrifice, for the good of those whom they

* We are even averse from examining natives as witnesses on the affairs of their own country. But three native witnesses were examined before the great Committee of the House of Commons on Indian finance. Yet, if the warnings they gave had been attended to, we should have reformed abuses in time to avert disaster in more than one district. Of course no one supposes that native evidence in regard to our rule is to be implicitly relied upon, but we ought at least to have some check upon the statements of officials as to their own capacity.

rule, but with their minds in England rather than in India.* With every wish to do their work thoroughly, to improve those for whom they are responsible, they soon find that they form part of an inexorable machine which grinds minutes, reports, and judgments out of them to such an extent that they have no time for friendly intercourse with the natives.

Here are some of the duties which fall upon a district officer, that district officer who is called by Dr. Hunter the real ruler of India. He is

Collector of the land revenue.
Registrar of the landed property in the district.
Judge between landlord and tenant.
Ministerial officer of the courts of justice.
Treasurer and accountant of the district.
Administrator of the district excise.
Ex-officio president of the local rates committee.
Referee for all questions of compensation for lands taken up for public purposes.
Agent for the Government in all local suits to which it is a party.
Referee in local public works.

* The late James Geddes was a notable instance of a man who may be said to have sacrificed his career and even his life to the welfare of the people he went out to rule. He preferred to state what he believed to be the truth rather than to attain to the highest offices by falling in with the prevailing opinion. A Bengal civilian of the first capacity, he ventured to doubt the beneficence of the system he was called upon to administer. He died a few months ago at the early age of forty, broken down by overwork and disappointment. Though his views may have been exaggerated and his suggestions not very practicable, no nobler character ever honoured the Indian services by participating in their work.

Manager of estates of minors.
Magistrate, police magistrate, and criminal judge.
Head of police.
Ex-officio president of municipalities.

There is, in fact, no real revenue administration. "The collector, especially in Oude and the Punjab, is a tax-gatherer and nothing more; he is compulsory jack-of-all-trades, whose days are spent in indicting countless reports on all miscellaneous matter of great or small importance upon which the local government of the day sets, or is forced to set, great store; he has to draw up portentous memos on conservancy, municipalities, drains, and self-government all the morning; his afternoons are occupied with his appellate work; and an odd half-hour or so, as leisure permits, is with difficulty snatched for the real work of a collector, namely, the disposal of the revenue reports—those papers which have to do with the future prosperity or ruin of whole villages." *

The all-important question of raised or increased assessment or remission—namely, the very hinge on which the whole welfare of the district hangs—"must be perfunctorily rushed through, while a proposal for a new latrine has taken up hours of valuable time." Overwhelmed, in short, with clerk work about matters of no moment, the collector has no opportunity for thoroughly getting to the bottom of his duties. Can any one wonder that, in such circumstances, the commonplace man is content to go on in the ordinary humdrum way; and that the man of ability, when he does get to the top of the

* "Our Land Revenue Policy in Northern India," by C. J. Connell, Bengal Civil Service.

tree, has all the ardour for reform taken out of him, and is only eager to get home? How can either acquire that intimate knowledge which is so essential, whilst he is hearing cases or compiling reports? The pressure of the bureaucracy is ever on him, and sooner or later he has to give in.

This, perhaps, is one of the most perplexing points in the future of our connection with India. Although India has known no other rule than ours for at least three generations, we are getting further and further from the people, and are less intimate with them than we were. This arises from various causes, some of which cannot be removed. But the excess of office work certainly does much mischief, and the constant transfers and frequent furloughs do more. On this serious difficulty the following remarks from a private letter to me may be interesting :—

"It is in general sadly true that Englishmen in India live totally estranged from the people among whom they are sojourning. This estrangement *is partly* unavoidable, being the result of national customs, language, and caste. But on the whole there is no doubt, I think, that it might in great part be removed if Englishmen would make up their minds (but how can they be ordered to do so?) to assume a less contemptuous attitude. Some natives in some respects *are* (it must be admitted) contemptible; but not all, or nearly all. We may say that while there is fault on both sides, the greater fault is on our side, because we have not performed a duty —clearly laid upon us by the nature of our position in India—of striving to understand the natives. The English contempt proceeds in the main from

English ignorance, and English ignorance is accompanied, as so often happens, by English bluster. Those who have known the natives well have generally liked them, even loved them, and their love has been returned with a remarkable wealth of unselfish affection. That natives are worth the effort of knowing, no humane person can doubt; but because with the difference of language and habits it *does* take some effort to know them, most Englishmen keep aloof. This tendency to aloofness is greater than it used to be, and is, I fear, increasing. This is a great misfortune. Some think that the increased tendency comes from an increase of Europeans of a lower social order than those who formerly came to India. It may be so; if so it can only be regarded and deplored as a new (but necessary) order of things. Certain it is the natives consider the Sahib is not what he used to be—certain, too, that English rule is not popular.

"This is the great social calamity attending our Raj in India. For it is not easy to dictate a remedy. Nothing can be effected by preaching or exhortation. The examples of Englishmen placed in high office may do and have done something to foster good-will between the different races; but the respect due to high office necessarily involves some formality, and forbids the expression of cordial sentiments. On the whole, nothing tangible can be achieved till the ordinary Englishman begins by treating the ordinary native as worthy to be known, and treats him, when found worthy, as an equal and a friend. But that happy day has not come yet. The army of the 'damned nigger' philistines is strong."

I may add that my friend, who is an Englishman. and an official, takes a much more favourable view of the present condition of India than I do.

Without, however, going further into detail, is it not abundantly clear that, so far as the main principles of our future administration are concerned, what we need is to remove from our own officials this excessive pressure of bureau work, and from the natives the excessive pressure of Europeans and European ideas, and European taxation above them? This can only be done by gradually reconstructing an improved native administration. The highest posts must, under one name or another, be in our hands so long as we remain in the country; but when we once admit that more native administration is desirable on all grounds, we shall have really begun that re-organisation which must be the work of the future.

The chief points to be always kept in view, indeed, in addition to relentless economy in India and at home, should be decentralisation, European supervision, native administration. Decentralisation, because it is utterly impossible—it is the root of many great grievances now—to rule well and tax fairly many nations and peoples on one distinct and definite plan. European supervision, because if we have no intention whatever of leaving the country, that is the best way of applying our superior knowledge. Native administration, because in this way alone shall we stanch in part the drain of produce, and give to the more capable natives that outlet for their capacities without which they will never be content, because also in this way alone shall we give free scope to those native arts and manufactures which at present are being crushed out under our system. Thus will the great provinces into which India is divided be prepared very gradually but very surely for that self-government which will be the noblest outcome of our rule. That India might be benefited by the English connection is undoubted; but it will be by guidance and help, not by stunting all spontaneous growth under a dead weight of Europeanisation.

To take the Public Works first. The Committee appointed by the House of Commons in 1879 fully confirmed the criticisms which I ventured to make upon the management of that department in 1878. A more damaging statement, calmly worded though it is, it would be difficult to find, or, it may be added, a more direct contradiction to the optimist statements of successive Secretaries and Under-Secretaries of State for India. For from that report it appears that up to the date of the inquiry £95,000,000 had been spent upon guaranteed railways; but, in addition to this capital expenditure, not less than £22,000,000 have been sent from India to England to meet the guaranteed interest which was never earned. On State railways at that time £18,600,000 had been spent, but as the money was borrowed at 4¼ per cent., and the railways cost about 3½ per cent., the sum paid, which was not earned on account of these railways, is still larger than the guaranteed railways in comparison with the total expended and the time during which the system has been in vogue. The loss to India on the State railways has been upwards of £2,000,000. By counting the East India Railway as a State Railway the loss disappears in the current year; but of course that is merely a matter of book-keeping—the loss is still incurred.

Thus on guaranteed and State railways there had been remitted to England—sticking still to the Report—£24,000,000, which had never been earned. What is more, every additional million spent on State railways means a further heavy loss to the State. As to the guaranteed railways, they did show a balance on the right side in 1877-78. But why? Simply because there was a frightful famine in Madras and Bombay, and enormous amounts of grain had to be sent from northern India to the suffering districts. Will it be believed that in this terrible year, when, notwithstanding the expenditure of £11,000,000 on famine relief, 6,000,000 people died of starvation, a 'bonus' was paid out of the produce of India to English shareholders? Yet so it was, though the very next year the loss on guaranteed interest figured as usual against the people of India.

Now in such circumstances what should be done? Surely borrowing should be stopped altogether, even if England, which has really been responsible for all this blundering, had to pay some of the unemployed officials. For consider even the cost of management in the Public Works Department. According to Sir Thomas Seccombe the outlay on establishments was actually £2,200,000, or enough to deal with an annual expenditure of £47,000,000. The proportion on our annual rate would be about 25 per cent. In Jeypore, as Sir James Caird pointed out, the cost of establishments under a European officer amounts to about 6 per cent. on the outlay. What makes all this the more sad is that, owing to the employment of so many Europeans in working the railroads, and the maintenance of the head offices in this country, they confer far less benefit than they otherwise would on the impoverished people. Yet borrowing for these 'productive' public works is still to go on, though it is quite impossible to insure that it will not increase the 'drain' for unearned interest, and still further weaken India. The same system, I say, is to go on, but on a smaller scale. Manifest as is the mistake, none will as yet fully acknowledge it.

In respect to irrigation works a different tone has fortunately been adopted. These, with the exception of a few native works restored or remodelled, are acknowledged to be a loss to the State, and no more are to be built with borrowed money, though loans for wells and tanks are recommended.

But in the face of this report and the very doubtful tone in which the committee speak about the whole of our public works in India, what becomes of those unfortunate illusions as to the results of our expenditure in this direction in India? The excess of European agency in every direction, the fact that the railways have been built with money borrowed out of the country, on which interest was paid whether earned or not—these two causes together have entirely vitiated the calculations made with regard to the ordinary benefit derived from such works. One of the poorest countries in the world has been saddled with expensive machinery of communication, from which the English investor derives the greatest benefit. Take, then, what view we may of what has already been done, further doubtful works ought only to be built from savings.

The Commissions which sat in England and in India with reference to the Indian army, will certainly report in favour of economy. But the main mischief was done, as has been pointed out time after time, when the amalgamation of the Indian and English armies was carried through, in opposition to the opinion of every man who had a right to express one. What is even more to the purpose, this was brought about, as Mr. Fawcett said, under a Liberal Government; and thus both sides are pledged to such changes as may remedy the mischief, including the reduction of the inordinate charge for retired colonels.

The Indian Commission of 1879 recommended the re-establishment of a local European force, recruited, officered, and pensioned on Indian account on reasonable terms. This plan was certain to meet with opposition in this country, and the drawbacks have frequently been pointed out by professional critics. That there were errors in the management of the old East India Company's local army was urged by none with more energy than by the eminent men of that army themselves. But that is no reason why they should be reproduced in any new arrangement The army would of course still be at the disposal of the Imperial authorities in case of emergency, only its first duty will be towards India. In this way the cost of transport will be greatly reduced, a long service army of thoroughly seasoned men would be maintained in the country at far less expense, the depôt charges in England would be cut down to something like the old scale under the East India Company, and such disorganisation as has lately been brought about by the attempt to apply the short service system of the Continent in totally different conditions would be avoided. Unfortunately the Commission has come to the conclusion that neither now nor later can the number of European troops in India be brought below 60,000. This, though possibly a right, is certainly a regrettable decision ; for the European force is that which inflates the military charges of India so inordinately.

If the question is asked, Why, when the Afghan war was over, was not the army reduced ? the reply is, Look at the danger from the native princes. An extraordinary array has been made of the armies of our feudatories, and 300,000 or 400,000 men with hundreds of guns have been paraded up and down the columns of English journals, as if some new or unsuspected peril had suddenly been flashed upon us. Such 'scares' are both impolitic and silly. They fill the native princes with an undue sense of their own importance, and at the same time give them the impression that we wish to treat them unfairly. If we really have ground to distrust the native States—and it is possible, though it seems most unlikely, that disaffection exists at Hyderabad, Gwalior, Indore, or elsewhere—we ought to act with promptitude and vigour. If not, then fair proposals should be made to our feudatories themselves to modify the treaties under which these useless forces are maintained before they are put forward as bogeys to frighten the English public at home. No one would argue that we are bound to permit native armies to be kept up in perpetuity which we have to tax our own fellow-subjects to pay the cost of watching, whilst the chiefs are themselves protected by us from any external attack or internal rising. But we have definite engagements, and these must honourably be dealt with by direct negotiations with the chiefs themselves. To act otherwise is only to provoke disaffection. Granting, however, that a satisfactory arrangement is made, and that definite peace is the result of our costly war in Afghanistan, then surely 50,000 European troops ought to suffice to garrison India. Nor is there any reason why, if the home charges are fairly apportioned and proper economy used, the cost of the army should exceed £13,000,000 in any one year.

When the license tax was imposed, Sir John Strachey justified the taxation of the very poorest of the population for the means of a provision against famine, on the ground that they first suffered from famine, and therefore ought to find the means for their own relief. The result of this strange reasoning was soon seen. The license tax produced more disaffection than any tax that has ever been imposed in India, and in some districts had a most disastrous effect. No wonder. The agriculturist was treated as an agriculturist, and had to pay all taxes as such; but the moment he moved his grain with his own cart and his own bullocks he became a trader, and had to pay in that capacity. Now this has been altered, and the license tax takes the form of an income tax —in itself no doubt an objectionable impost, but not, like the other, a direct incitement to disaffection. Surely it is high time that this tinkering with the interests of our empire should be put an end to, and more consideration shown for the mass of the people.

For it is not only with the license tax that the most serious harm has been done. "Arrears" are still being exacted—arrears for years during which the land produced nothing at all, when, indeed, the economical rent of which we have heard so much might be taken to represent a minus quantity. At the same time, too, the increased salt tax, against which the Madras Government so strenuously protested, has been imposed and is being demanded. The result of course is that even during these years of comparative plenty the agricultural classes are still in want and misery. On such points it is for the Home Government to express a decided opinion, and to rescue the oppressed. For the grave mischief of all this is that the difficulties of one year become hopeless calamity the next.

To crush the poor and spare the wealthy has been almost the rule with the Indian Government of late years. A change has begun ; let us hope it will be pushed on vigorously.

Of the details of Indian finance it is needless now to speak at length. That the condition of the Exchequer is deplorable is now universally admitted. What is still more serious, the improvement of the revenue in certain directions may as well be considered "accidental" as the exceptional expenditure on war or famine, whilst the depletion of the cash balances has been carried to such an extent as to be positively dangerous. Further borrowing —that easy resort of the spendthrift—has been rendered necessary to an extent which must alarm even the most careless. Nothing short of a close and careful scrutiny of the whole fabric of our Indian finances will now suffice to convince the public that they rest on a sound basis. The time has gone by when any set of tables, however carefully manipulated, will carry conviction. Once more the flattering estimates of an Indian Finance Minister, even apart from the miscalled productive expenditure, turned out wholly delusive, and this time we may reasonably hope that the blunder cannot be passed over as a trivial error. For now the English people will themselves have to put their hands in their pockets to rectify the mistaken calculations of the Indian Government, and thus they will have a direct interest in finding out the truth. But there remain graver facts for consideration than any affected by the deficit of the current year. Though we passed through one famine period at the cost of millions of lives and millions of money, with the loss of numbers of cattle, and serious general impoverishment of the districts affected, within a few years we must come to another time of dearth, and for this period no preparation whatever is now being made.

All the discussion which has taken place on this question, all the efforts of the supporters of the present Finance Minister, cannot alter the fact that the £1,500,000 of surplus that was to have been provided by extra taxation in order to anticipate the needs of the people has been used for the Afghan War and frontier railways. Try how we may to turn the figures about, the truth remains that the Famine Insurance Fund, the necessary annual amount to make ready for the next period of drought, or by judicious investment to give facilities for borrowing at the critical moment, has been utterly swept away, and more and yet more debt incurred. What need have we of further argument when we see for ourselves that borrowing could not even be delayed, so heavy was the pressure? Yet the grave dangers to which we were exposed are grave dangers still. The people are miserably poor, taxation cannot be increased without great risk, and the drain of produce which goes relentlessly on is producing—let that never be forgotten—a cumulative effect. Period for period, therefore, each successive year is worse than its predecessor, and does but bring the final catastrophe nearer to us.

As regards the mere question of finance in itself, there is also the opium revenue to be considered. This even now is not so secure as it was. Every step which China takes towards organising her naval and military forces renders this source of income less certain; whilst all the time there is a party here at home which to do a little right would risk a great wrong, and crush the Indian taxpayer rather than sell to the Chinaman what they consider a harmful drug. The arguments put forward by the moralists who wish to give up the Indian opium revenue are based, we may suppose, upon the idea that the amount of revenue thus sacrificed could be raised with equal convenience in some other way; or at least that retrenchments could be made which would render some £7,000,000 of revenue unnecessary. But no effort whatever is made to show how this sum could be obtained in India, nor do the enthusiasts point out where proportionate economies might be effected in the expenditure. As a matter of fact, £7,000,000 of additional revenue could not be obtained in India, and he would be a financier indeed who should show the way to a genuine surplus of that amount. The truth is also that, though there is nothing to be said for the manner in which we forced the opium traffic upon China, opium smoking is far less harmful in every way than dram drinking, and, as was observed not long since, Indian opium holds much the same position with respect to native Chinese opium that fine French brandy does to fusel-oil gin. India, in short, has a monopoly of the one, as France has of the other, and we use it to lighten Indian taxation. Find a substitute which shall not oppress our fellow-subjects, or curtail expenditure *pro tanto*, and then the Indian Government can afford to give ear to the member for Glasgow, the sobriety of his constituents notwithstanding. Here alone is a danger which sooner or later must be faced and dealt with. India positively could not raise the additional £6,000,000 or £7,000,000 needed to replace the net opium revenue. Thus, then, the permanent causes of uneasiness are still unshaken, and the little which has been done already is rather an assurance for the future than a ground for confidence at present.

A leading article actually appeared in the *Times* which would appear to show that India, so far from being impoverished, is steadily advancing in wealth. This conclusion was arrived at by comparing the export and import trade of India in 1869-70 with the export and import trade, so far as known, in 1879-80. The article was written *à propos* of the statement of the Chairman of the Calcutta Chamber of Commerce to the effect that the outlook for the Indian export trade is very gloomy indeed, and that there is little likelihood that it will be any better in years to come. In reply to that statement the *Times* shows that the export trade of India between 1870 and 1880 has increased 20 per cent.; and the import of merchandise 25 per cent., and then urges with apparent justice that when the trade thus increases India cannot be getting poorer. The consideration of the trade of India had been purposely excluded, for I thought that it had been sufficiently dealt with in previous papers, and that the admission of a Finance Minister that £20,000,000 of agricultural produce—it is really over £30,000,000, but let that pass—leaves India every year without any direct commercial equivalent, was enough to show that India did not derive any benefit, but on the contrary suffered severe loss, from her export and import trade.

The argument of the *Times*, however, calls for some notice. I would therefore point out that between 1870 and 1880 the mileage of railroads open in India had been increased not 20 or 25, but nearly 100 per cent., that there is therefore twice the facility for communication with the seaboard at the least, and certainly twice the extent of country opened up to foreign trade in 1880 that there was in 1870. The increase of trade might well be proportionate. It is not so, nor nearly so. But this increase of trade, such as it is, must be in fairness attributed wholly to the new districts. What then becomes of the trade from the country already opened up in 1870? That, I venture to affirm, has decreased on the average; and I venture further to predict that the anticipations of the Chairman of the Calcutta Chamber of Commerce will be only too sadly fulfilled unless we alter our system.

I would further point out that if the importers of merchandise are scrutinised or larger imports questioned, it will be found that the natives of India in our own territory are importing no luxuries, —the imported cotton of course means the destruction by greater cheapness of native industries,—though during the one period when they had anything to spare (the cotton famine time) they bought European articles readily enough. In estimating, therefore, the export and import trade of India, it is necessary to bear in mind that not only are all the prosperous European ventures of which the profits are ours, not only is all the trade of the Native States included in the returns, but that the enormous increase of railway communication has practically opened up twice the country that was within profitable reach of the seaboard ten years ago. It is not pleasant to have to admit that a country under our direct rule is becoming poorer and poorer; but it is useless to shut our eyes to plain facts, however disagreeable they may be. That way lies ruin.

The drawbacks to our rule since the Mutiny are only too apparent, their effects only too grievous. Yet all these can—all these must be—remedied. The alternative—what would almost certainly occur if we were to leave India before we had finished the task of remedying our blunders, and of reorganising a country which under good administration would be one of the richest and most flourishing portions of the earth—is not pleasant to contemplate. Natives of India, broken up as they are into many races and religions, would never be content to settle down each to the peaceful management of their own. We have enforced peace, order, general security, but we have not yet built up—have not even tried to build up—any native system fit to take our place. What, then, would ensue? A savage contest between Mahommedan and Mahratta, Sikh and Pathan, for the supremacy of the country. Our controlling influence removed, all the elements of disorder would burst forth and have free play.

Railways would be torn up, tanks broached, cities sacked, the Nepaulese and other hill tribes would descend again into the plains, and the condition of India in this nineteenth century of ours would be worse than if we had never entered it.

For this intestine strife would not be the end: other European States would take advantage of all the turmoil to thrust its yoke upon the conflicting natives, and to renew in a yet sterner shape the mischievous system from which we at least should be willing to set it free. Therefore we are bound to go on. But, this being so, it becomes the duty of every man to take care that the next twenty years shall not be as the last, that India shall not longer be regarded as the preserve of any clique or class, and that persistent optimism or indifference shall not blind us to the hard reality of facts and figures. The great mass of English voters are now the real masters of India—it is for them to see that only worthy deeds are done in their name.

Even as we look on, India is becoming feebler and feebler. The very lifeblood of the great multitude under our rule is slowly, yet ever faster, ebbing away. Listen then no more to those comfortable counsellors who, in the face of the fatal truths day by day made manifest, delude us with their idle talk of growing strength, of increasing prosperity, of healthful national vigour in the near future, when all the while the great dependency we are responsible for is perishing from exhaustion, because we drag from her helplessness millions worth of agricultural produce which she cannot spare. Further delay to act in this matter simply means that the number of those who will die of starvation at the next scarcity will be hideously multiplied by our default, that the certainty of their fate is assured by our neglect. A policy of steady retrenchment at home, and in India of greatly increased employment of natives and careful reconstruction of native governments, may be no easy one to carry out ; but this way lies the future of India, and thus alone shall we earn the gratitude of generations to come.

IV.

CONTINUED NEGLECT.

SINCE the last of the three previous chapters was written, more than six years have elapsed—six eventful years in the history of our connection with India. Unfortunately the promise of reform given immediately after their publication by a Conservative Government has not been fulfilled. The cost of the two Afghan wars, with the exception of £5,000,000, as well as a large portion of the cost of the war in Egypt, has been thrown upon the revenues of India; the economies made at that time in the extravagant Public Works Department have been entirely neglected, and all the old shameful jobbery and nepotism goes on as before; the recommendations of the Famine Commission and the warnings of Sir James Caird have passed almost unheeded; the endeavour of Lord Ripon, trifling as it was, to give the natives a greater share in the government of their own country, was defeated by the selfish clamour of official and non-official Anglo-Indians; a war of annexation of the old unscrupulous type has been carried on in Burmah, for the benefit of Anglo-Indian placemen and mercantile adventurers, with the consent of both parties; the debt has been enormously increased without protest; there is still an outcry for the further "development" of our great dependency by English capital, ruinous though such development has been shown to be; and last, not least, 10,000 men have been added to our already costly military establishment in India.

Meanwhile, owing to this policy of deliberate indifference, the impoverishment of the agricultural population has become more terrible; and the bankruptcy of India, which eight years ago had been recognised only by the late Mr. Geddes, Mr. Dadabhai Naoroji and myself, as one of the most threatening features of our future economical history, is now looked forward to with alarm even by Finance Ministers, and is being seriously dealt with as a difficulty of the day. No wonder. Deficit succeeds deficit with monotonous regularity, and the efforts made by the clique of Anglo-Indian bureaucrats in Parliament and in the press to hide away the facts from their long-suffering countrymen, are no longer quite so successful as they were.

Unfortunately, Englishmen of the working classes have not yet understood the importance to them, even from a selfish point of view, of the well-being of the people of India. A starving ryot cannot buy even Lancashire cotton goods. Yet we deliberately destroy one of our best markets by impoverishing our own customers. Who benefits by the vast wealth derived annually from India without return? Not the English workers assuredly. Go to Blackburn, Oldham, Rochdale, and other headquarters of the Indian cotton-trade; are the factory hands there so well off? Not they. They work in bad conditions of existence for low wages, while those who buy their goods are going from bad to worse. More pressing than ever then is the need that the plain facts should once more be set out.

FINANCE.

The official statement of a nation's finances may often be no very accurate test of its real economical position. Much may be done in the way of cooking figures, much more may be effected by the careful squeezing of the people, which tends to obscure the real state of the case below. Thus it is possible for unscrupulous financiers, by means of loans and other devices, to tide over the evil day of reckoning for many years. Nevertheless, the mass of the people may be getting poorer, in spite of all the apparent prosperity, and the eventual collapse will only be the more dangerous from the determination to evade the publication of the truth. This is precisely the case with India, though a careful analysis of the successive Budgets is by itself enough to cause uneasiness. That the country is heavily taxed, notwithstanding all the nonsense talked by interested panegyrists, has already been clearly shown. Close on £75,000,000, taken in one form or another for State purposes from a people whose total gross income is put at £300,000,000 on a fair, and at £400,000,000 by an optimist calculation, is in itself a statement sufficiently startling to arrest the attention of all save those who deliberately refuse to understand. On the same lines the annual taxation of Great Britain and Ireland would be £300,000,000; and even this would be much less heavy in proportion, in the same way that £250 a year out of an income of £1,000 a year is a trifling matter compared with the sacrifice of £7 10s. on £30 a year. Nor does the fact that a portion of the revenue is derived from the proceeds of the railways lessen the pressure; for the sums thus taken in the form of profit are remitted to England to pay interest, and thus constitute as distinct a deduction from the gross produce as the amounts taken from India to pay away in pensions.

India, therefore, is very heavily taxed in proportion to its means. Taking the average income per family of five persons at £8, then £2 is taken for the purposes of government. But as Bengal is not so heavily taxed as other districts in proportion to its wealth, the weight of taxation over the rest of India is heavier than this. It is true that of late years the salt tax has been slightly reduced in some districts and equalised all over India; true, too, that the cotton duties have been removed in the sole interest of the Manchester manufacturers. But these measures have certainly not produced any marked improvement in the condition of the people; nor do the statements of successive Finance Ministers, that each fresh deficit is the result of unforeseen causes, alter the fact that they are at their wits' end to make both ends meet, or disguise the disagreeable truth that the debt of India is perpetually growing, while the imposition of much heavier taxation is practically out of the question.

For all the time the main heads of revenue, excepting the receipts from public works, remain practically stationary. Land, salt, opium, excise stamps, certainly do not show that elasticity which would justify us in the continual borrowing to which we resort. Simultaneously the fall in the price of silver occasions an increasing loss by exchange, which has at length frightened the Government of India into advocating some attempt to raise its price by artificial means. Any sudden emergency must be met, of course, by additional loans, and these emergencies, in a great empire like India, form the rule rather than the exception.

Nor is there any reason to hope that the Home Charges which occasion this loss by remittance will decrease. If the rupee is reckoned at 2*s.*, and the home charges amount to £17,000,000 or £18,000,000, which is now the average, it needs no great arithmetician to discover that a fall of the rupee to an average value of 1*s.* 6*d.* or even 1*s.* 4*d.*, calls for a remittance of upwards of one-third more if the same ratio is kept up ; and that, consequently, the "loss" in any given year *may* amount to £6,000,000 or £7,000,000. How far our economical relations with India tend to aggravate this serious disturbing element in our calculations it is unnecessary to enlarge upon again here ; but, taken in connection with the possibility of a check to the opium revenue, not the most enthusiastic optimist can deny that the situation is exceedingly perilous. Nor should we overlook the complicated character of our foreign exchanges, which any shake in this quarter might altogether unhinge.

The present Finance Minister having a deficit, notwithstanding the imposition of the income-tax, speaks with positive dread of the effects of a continued fall in silver upon the budget, which he is obliged to balance by a large draft upon the already depleted Provincial Revenues. No suggestion, however, does he make for the reduction of the terrible home charges, which cause all the mischief. In the year 1884, for instance, the Secretary of State drew bills on India to the nominal amount of £21,621,546 at 2*s.* the rupee, the proceeds of which were £17,599,805, or an apparent loss of £4,021,741!

To show how these drawings and consequent losses have increased, it is almost sufficient to state that the drawings were in round figures £86,000,000, or £7,160,000 a year nominal, in the twelve years between 1862 and 1873 inclusive, and the rupee fetching over 1*s.* 11*d.* on the average, the total loss was comparatively trifling. The following table shows the increase in the eleven years 1874-1884 inclusive.

YEAR.	RUPEES.	£		£
1874 . .	14,26,57,000	13,285,678	1 10·351	980,022
1875 . .	11,74,37,000	10,841,615	1 10·156	902,085
1876 . .	13,75,00,000	12,389,613	1 9·625	1,360,387
1877 . .	14,85,75,122	12,695,799	1 8·508	2,161,713
1878 . .	11,69,85,000	10,134,455	1 8·791	1,564,045
1879 . .	16,91,23,612	13,948,565	1 7·794	2,963,796
1880 . .	18,35,00,000	15,261,810	1 7·961	3,088,190
1881 . .	18,32,77,000	15,239,677	1 7·956	3,088,023
1882 . .	22,21,09,350	18,412,429	1 7·895	3,798,506
1883 . .	18,58,56,593	15,120,521	1 7·525	3,465,138
1884 . .	21,62,15,462	17,599,805	1 7·536	4,021,741

Here, too, at last is the long-asked-for return of the amount of annual salaries paid in and out of India.

RESIDENT.	£	s.	d.
17,093 Salaries	6,811,422	15	0
1,725 Pensions	679,079	16	0
430 Gratuities and Absentee Allowances	149,670	8	3
	£7,640,172	19	3

NON-RESIDENT.	£	s.	d.
7,660 Annuities, Furlough Pay, etc. .	3,069,565	0	0
865 Home Establishments	403,800	0	0
	£3,473,365	0	0

Here we have then a yearly grand total of upwards of £11,000,000, nearly all paid to Europeans in and out of India. To quote a recent writer, "for salaries and soldiers in British India nearly three-fifths of the net revenue is appropriated"! Of that amount only about one-fifth is spent in the country. The expenditure in England for interest on debt for Public Works, etc., amounts now to fully £15,000,000 nominal on the average. Surely then Finance Ministers might look a little more closely into the facts instead of raising a general wail about the fall in the price of silver, as if that were the sole cause of financial difficulty. For, all the while, the expenditure on Public Works, Productive (so-called) and Ordinary, goes steadily on at the rate of from £10,000,000 to £12,000,000 a year, of which expenditure one-fourth is paid away in salaries to Europeans.

Leaving a closer examination of recent expenditure in this direction until later, it is still more clear now than it was six years ago, that India cannot afford such a frightfully extravagant system of government as that which has paid away no less than £17,000,000 a year, and now intends to spend more, on its army in time of peace; and likewise pays away for military services and civil salaries £24,000,000 out of a total net revenue of £40,000,000. Such waste as this from the revenues of a poor country can have but one ending. The increase of the total debt to £250,000,000, of which not a tenth is held by natives should alone check the exuberance of Anglo-Indian apologists. Although there has been no great famine during the last few years, the truth already set forth still remains unshaken, that the soil, the people, the cattle of India, are undergoing steady but increasingly rapid deterioration, and that no steps of any importance are being taken to check the speedy progress of decay. It is scarcely too much to say that, having been awakened for a moment by the fearful mortality in Bombay, Madras, and the North-West Provinces in the years 1877, '78, and '79, the public of England has gone to sleep again, and will never be aroused from its slumber of indifference until a still more terrible affliction falls upon our fellow-subjects. The more reason why the facts relating to that visitation should be recalled, now that we have reached a period when the recurrence of famine cannot long be deferred.

FAMINES.

It was in the year 1878 that the Secretary of State for India appointed a Famine Commission to inquire into the causes of these great dearths, and to suggest means of averting or remedying them. By far the most important member of that Commission was Sir James Caird, to whose appointment special reference has been already made; and it is scarcely necessary to repeat that he went out to India convinced, as he stated in the *Times*, that the view which I hold of the condition of our great dependency was entirely a mistaken one. His investigations on the spot completely undeceived him. On his return this skilled expert confirmed almost everything which I had alleged as to the dangers ahead of us, and threw overboard altogether the attempts of his official colleagues to prove that all was for the best in the best of dependencies possible.

Sir James Caird's separate Report to the Secretary of State for India was dated October 31st, 1879, when he was still fresh from his tour through our provinces, and contains the following striking passages:—

"The available good land in India is nearly all occupied. There are extensive areas of good waste land covered with jungle in various parts of the country, which might be reclaimed and rendered suitable for cultivation, but for that object capital must be employed, and the people have little to spare.* The produce of the country on an average of years is barely sufficient to maintain the present population, and make a saving for occasional famine. The greatest export of rice and corn in one year is not more than ten days' consumption of its inhabitants. Scarcity, deepening into famine, is thus becoming of more frequent occurrence." Scarcity, deepening into famine, is thus becoming of more frequent occurrence! Yet we are told to congratu-

* Such clearances would besides affect the rainfall injuriously, and still further promote drought.

late ourselves all round upon the beneficial effects of our rule in India.

"The people may be assumed to increase at the moderate rate of one per cent. per year.* The check caused by the late famine through five million of extra deaths,"—there were really more than seven million of extra deaths; but let that pass,—"spread, as it was, over two years and a half, would thus be equal only to the nominal increase over all India for that time." In ten years, at the present rate of growth, there will be twenty millions more people to feed, in twenty years upwards of forty millions. This must be met by an increase of produce, arising from better management of the cultivated area, and enlargement of its extent by emigration to unpeopled districts, and by emigration to other countries. We are dealing with a country already full of people, whose habits and religion promote increase without restraint, and whose law directs the sub-division of land among all the male children. As rulers, we are thus brought face to face with a growing difficulty. *There are more people every year to feed from land which, in many parts of India, is undergoing gradual deterioration.* Of this there can be no stronger proof than that the land revenue in some quarters is diminishing. It is unsafe to break up more of the uncultivated low land. The diminution of pasture thereby already caused is showing its effect in a lessening proportion of working cattle for an increasing area of cultivation."

Does not that passage bear out everything which has been previously urged as to the serious dangers

* The real increase is ·68 per cent. per annum.

ahead of us? Can any sober Englishman read through the sentence in italics without a dread of coming disaster? Moreover, "the pressure on the means of subsistence is rendered more severe by the moral disorganisation produced by laws affecting property and debts not adapted to the people. . . . Those British officials who see this feel themselves powerless to influence a central authority for removal from, subject to no control of public opinion, and overburdened with details with which it is incapable of dealing." Legislation, in fact, steps jauntily in to complete the ruin which economical causes have begun. A pretty state of things to feel happy about, truly.

Sir James Caird goes on to denounce our "centralising system," the thoughtless manner in which we have ousted native authority, and helped to break up the old native forms by needless Europeanisation. Yet "our officers"—note how precisely this statement corresponds with the views already set forth at p. 137—"our officers do not know the natives as they used to do when our Government was less centralised, and they are every year becoming more strange to the people by the increase of indoor judicial duties, and the frequent changes from one locality to another." I pass over the portion of the report which deals with the rigidity of our exactions, and the methods by which the cultivator has been "made the slave of the money-lender." It is enough to quote two sentences: "Having parted with those two sheet-anchors, the native village organisation, and the self-adjusting principle of land tenure with produce rents, Indian statecraft has fallen upon the quicksands of legal chicanery. In consequence of this, at much cost to the State, a large proportion of official strength is kept constantly engaged upon questions of law which harass and impoverish the people." Produce rents are not essential by any means, where a light assessment is considerately collected. But the rest is unfortunately too true.

Then the perils of reassessment and the mischiefs of excessive exaction are again insisted upon. But the gravest difficulties are those of population and decreasing fertility of the soil. Once more, therefore, let us hear Sir James Caird in this report: "It must be constantly borne in mind, in considering this question, that a large portion of the population of India are now of the labouring class, dependent on employment, and the more the land becomes subdivided, and then more exclusively cultivated by its possessor, the more dependent becomes the position of the landless labourer. Though wages have risen at the centres of industry, this is not the case in the purely agricultural parts of the country. In such localities the labourer gets the same dole that he got in the last generation. The numbers of such people are increasing, and their condition is becoming every ten years more desperate."

"Thus the greatest difficulty with which the Indian statesman is confronted is overpopulation, with constant increase, and his first and main duty will be to carry out a policy under which the people may be enabled to supply themselves with food,"—doubtless seeing that it is the necessary condition of their continued existence. "Every consideration should be subordinate to this." . . .

"The agricultural system, except in the richer and irrigated lands, is to eat or sell every saleable article the land produces, to use the manure of the cattle for fuel, and to return nothing to the soil in any proportion to what is taken away. Every increase of population aggravates the danger. When population was not pressing on the cultivated land, and there was space enough to admit of it, the exhausted land was allowed to rest in fallow for a time, and in the hot sun and genial rains to recruit its productive powers. But there is no room longer for this. Crop follows crop without intermission, so that Indian agriculture is becoming simply a process of exhaustion. Even in some tracts of canal-irrigated land, where water is lavishly used, without manure crops have ceased to grow. An exhausting agriculture and an increasing population must come to a deadlock. No reduction of the assessment can be more than a postponement of the inevitable catastrophe, and no attempt by the Government or its officers merely to shift the burden will avert the two-fold difficulty. The task of government is thus one of enormous difficulty unless we are prepared to leave the surplus population to be periodically cut down by famine to the numbers which a rude agriculture can maintain."

Do we need further evidence? "An exhausting agriculture and an increasing population must come to a dead-lock. No reduction of the assessment can be more than a postponement of the inevitable catastrophe." Can anything add force to those sentences written by a cool Scotch agriculturist and Government official of Liberal opinions, sent out specially to examine into the facts by a Conservative administration ?

The Government of India tried, in a despatch printed with Sir James Caird's report, to whittle away the effect of these damning paragraphs. To no purpose. The facts are too plain, the conclusions too manifest. Nay, what is more, they are, as we shall shortly see, supported and enforced by Dr. W. W. Hunter, the Registrar-General of Indian Statistics. But in his dissent, in common with Mr. Sullivan, from the joint report of his fellow-commissioners, Sir James Caird once more endeavours to impress upon his countrymen the magnitude of the calamity which had then lately befallen India, thus: "The people of England can hardly realise the loss by death in the last Indian famine. Upwards of five millions of human beings, more in number than the population of Ireland, perished in that miserable time. If the people of this vast metropolis, with the millions in its neighbourhood, were all melted away by a lingering death, even this would not exceed in numbers the loss to India. A result so fearful in extent, and so heartrending in its details, was brought about by want of timely preparation to meet a calamity which, though irregular in its arrival, is periodical and inevitable."

This the following official table shows clearly :—

YEAR.	AREA OF DROUGHT.	AREA OF FAMINE OR SCARCITY.
1769	Drought in Bengal.	
1770	. . . .	Famine in Bengal.
1782	Drought in Bombay and Madras.	
1783	Drought in Upper India . .	Famine in Madras and scarcity in Bombay.
1784	. . . .	Famine in Upper India from the Karamnasa to the Sutlej.

YEAR.	AREA OF DROUGHT.	AREA OF FAMINE OR SCARCITY.
1791	Drought in Bombay, Hyderabad, and Madras.	
1792	. . . .	Scarcity in north part of Madras. Intense famine in Hyderabad and Southern Mahratta country. Severe famine in Deccan, Guzerat, and Marwar.
1802	Drought in South Hyderabad, and in Deccan.	
1803	Drought in Ceded Province of North-Western Provinces and in Central India . . .	Famine in Deccan and Hyderabad.
1804	. . . .	Famine in North-Western Provinces, and scarcity in Central India and Rajputana.
1806	Drought in Central Districts of Madras, from Trichinopoly to Nellore.	
1807	. . . .	Famine in Central Districts of Madras.
1812	Drought in Guzerat, Kutch, and Kathiawar, and to some extent in Madras; also in Rajputana and Central India.	
1813	. . . .	Famine in Kutch and Kathiawar; intense in parts of Rajputana. Scarcity in parts of North-Western Provinces and of Madras.
1823	Drought in Madras.	
1824	Drought in Bombay . . .	Famine in Madras, chiefly in the north.
1825	. . . .	Scarcity in Bombay, chiefly in Guzerat and the Northern Deccan.
1832	Drought in Northern districts of Madras, except Ganjam, in the south of Hyderabad, and the Southern Mahratta districts of Bombay.	
1833	Drought in north part of Bombay, in Rajputana, and parts of Punjab and North-Western Provinces	Famine in Northern districts of Madras; intense in Gantur. Scarcity in Hyderabad and Southern Mahratta districts.
1834	. . . . .	Scarcity in North Deccan and Guzerat, in Rajputana, the Hissar division of Punjab, and the trans-Jumna districts of North-Western Provinces.
1837	Drought in North-Western Provinces, Eastern States of Rajputana, and south-east part of Punjab.	

YEAR.	AREA OF DROUGHT.	AREA OF FAMINE OR SCARCITY.
1838	Drought in Guzerat, Kutch, and Kathiawar	Intense famine in Central Doab and trans-Jumna districts of North-Western Provinces, and in Delhi and Hissar divisions of Punjab.
1839	. . . .	Scarcity in Guzerat, Kutch, and Kathiawar.
1844	Scanty rainfall in Deccan.	
1845	. . . .	Scarcity in Deccan
1853	Drought in Ceded Districts of Madras, in South Hyderabad, and Sholapur and Kaladgi districts of Bombay.	
1854	. . . .	Famine in Bellary. Scarcity in adjoining parish of Madras, Hyderabad, and Bombay.
1860	Drought in part of North-Western Provinces and Punjab, and neighbouring States of Rajputana.	
1861	. . . .	Famine in Upper Doab of North-Western Provinces, in Delhi and Hissar divisions of Punjab, and in adjoining parts of Rajputana. Scarcity in Kutch.
1865	Drought in northern part of Madras, in South Hyderabad and north part of Mysore; in South Mahratta districts of Bombay, in Orissa and Behar, and all Western Bengal.	
1866	. . . .	Famine in Ganjam and Bellary districts of Madras, in Orissa (intense), and in Behar. Scarcity in all adjacent parts of Madras, Mysore, Hyderabad, and Bombay, and in Central and Western Bengal.
1868	Drought in Rajputana, trans-Jumna districts of North-Western Provinces, north and south-east districts of Central Provinces, and in Punjab from Jumna to Indus.	
1869	. . , . . .	Famine in Western Rajputana (intense), in trans-Jumna districts of Allahabad and Delhi, and Hissar divisions of Punjab. Scarcity in adjacent parts of North-Western Provinces and Punjab, in Guzerat, Kutch, and North Deccan, and in the north and south-east districts of Central Provinces.

YEAR.	AREA OF DROUGHT.	AREA OF FAMINE OR SCARCITY.
1873	Drought in North Behar and a part of North-Western Provinces and Oudh.	
1874	. . . .	Famine in Behar and scarcity in the strip of North-Western Provinces and Oudh adjacent.
1876	Drought in all Madras and Deccan, Mysore, and South part of Hyderabad.	
1877	Drought in Central Provinces, North-Western Provinces, and Punjab	Famine in Madras, Mysore, Bombay, and Hyderabad.
1878	. . . .	Famine in North-Western Province and Cashmere. Scarcity in Punjab.

The exceptional loss of life by famine since the beginning of the century cannot be put at less than 18,000,000, though the official returns, omitting several famines, make the mortality but 12,700,000. No wonder that, among other remedies, Sir James Caird suggested a reversion to the old native method of storage of grain. His answer to the contention of his official fellow-commissioners with reference to the surplus of food, which they said is annually produced in India, must be given in this connection :—

"We are unable to place confidence in the Table at page 50, which shows an estimated annual surplus yield of five million tons of food grain. The average annual export of rice and grain from all India is one million tons, which should thus leave four million tons to be laid by, a quantity sufficient to feed twenty-four millions of people. As famines come but once in twelve years, there should in that period be an accumulated surplus sufficient to feed nearly three hundred millions. And yet when famine does come, and then affecting at its worst not more than a tenth of that number, it is only by immense pressure on other parts of India, and at a quadrupled price, that the barest sufficiency of supplies can be obtained. This seems a clear proof that the alleged surplus must be greatly overestimated. Considering, also, the admittedly 'approximate and rough estimates' on which the belief in this surplus is based, and the exhausting practice of agriculture so generally followed in the cultivation of dry grain in India, we are unable to concur in the statement that 'India as a whole now produces, and is likely long to produce, sufficient food for its population in any season of drought.' The 'prolonged teachings of the past' referred to in the Report are, as far as that country is concerned, wholly against such a conclusion."

"Population is increasing, the price of food is rising, the production of it, as shown by exports, scarcely advances, whilst, as the number of the landless class who depend on wages is constantly growing, the supply of labour in the absence of industries other than agriculture must soon exceed the demand. Already their wages bear a less proportion to the price of food than in any country of which we have knowledge. The common price of grain in the Southern States of America on which the free black labourer is fed, is the same as that of the Indian labourer, viz., 50 to 60 lbs. per rupee. But his wages are eight times that of the Indian, 2*s.* to 2*s.* 3*d.*, against 3*d.* a day, whilst the climate is much the same in its demands for clothing and shelter. This is a fact of extreme gravity as illustrative of the poverty of the Indian coolie or field labourer, not to be met by resting satisfied that 'chronic famine is one of the diseases of the infancy of nations.' For India, as a nation, has long passed its 'infancy,' and the task of the British Government is, by fostering diversity of occupation, to guard it against decline."

I have said that these statements are in the main fully borne out by Dr. W. W. Hunter. The little book, "England's Work in India," in which he gives his opinion, is now out of print; but the official evidence of the head of the statistical department is so important, especially at the present time, that I need make no excuse for quoting what he says. He states that if "the food supply were equally distributed there would be plenty for all." This contention Sir James Caird has already disposed of, and in any case it would be well to show where the surplus supply of food goes to.

But a little lower down Dr. Hunter really throws overboard his own contention, seeing that, even taking his own very loose figures, he finds it necessary to add: "Two-fifths of the people of British India enjoy a prosperity unknown under native rule; other two-fifths earn a fair but diminishing subsistence; but the remaining fifth or forty millions go through life on insufficient food. It is these underfed forty millions who form the problem of over-population in India." And further on he says again, "Over-population in India is the direct product of British rule." This, I admit, he does not mean in the condemnatory sense, for he asserts that it is due to the suppression of infanticide, the maintenance of peace, and other similar causes.

Strange it is, nevertheless, that experts should so often overlook the well-known law that a poor population, other things remaining unchanged, tends to increase more rapidly as it becomes poorer until the famine stage is reached, though India and Ireland furnish the two most marked instances of its truth. But the result is the same, and those who, in view of these facts, can look hopefully to the future, if the present system is continued, are indeed sanguine or wilfully blind. It is childish to talk of reform and reconstruction while no attempt is made to check the progress of this impoverishment.

Our own officials are themselves, or the more able of them, beginning to see this. As, for example, Mr. H. T. S. Cotton, of the Bengal Civil Service, in a little book entitled "New India," recently published. He urges that "There is no great harm in saying that the land belongs to 'the State'"—he is speaking of the management of the Land Revenue—"when the State is only another name for the people; but it is a very different thing when the State is represented by a small minority of foreigners, who disburse nearly one-third of the revenues received from the land on the remuneration of their own servants, and who have no abiding-place on the soil and no stake in the fortunes of the country. It is because we have acted on this principle all over India, with the exception of the permanently settled districts, that we have reduced the country to such poverty." Surely that is a very strong statement. "By vigorously asserting the false principle that a party of foreign occupiers, who choose to call themselves 'the State'"—a party of foreign occupiers who choose to call themselves the State! Have I ever used stronger language than this Bengal Civilian?—"have become the proprietors of the actual soil of India, we have destroyed all other rights of property therein, from the talookdar down to the ryot; we have subverted the entire organisation of the village communities; we have torn up by the roots the economical fabric by which the agricultural classes of the country were held together, and we have substituted in its place a costly and mechanical centralisation."

After comparing our system most unfavourably with that of the Moguls in this respect, the official writer goes on: "If as surely as production increases the Government demand be increased also, it is impossible to expect that the peasantry will labour for the improvement of the land or the extension of cultivation. There is no sense of security which alone will attract capital and intelligence to agriculture. A bare margin for subsistence alone remains, and the result is that indebtedness extends year by year, and that famines recur with ever-increasing frequency and severity." Mr. Connell, in his excellent work on "Our Land Revenue Policy in Northern India," comes to the same conclusion, and it would be easy to cite other courageous official writers to the same effect.

But now come the proposals for remedying this state of things, and what do we find? Why, that Sir James Caird and Dr. W. W. Hunter, the Famine Commissioners, and the non-official writers, are all agreed that withdrawal of the people from agriculture to non-agricultural industries; migration and emigration; an increase of the produce of the existing area of cultivation; are the best means of improving the present state of things. But these, together with an extension of public works and storage of grain, can only be carried on by borrowing or by accumulation of produce—by capital borrowed or by capital saved. To borrow more money from England is to increase still further the already ruinous drain of produce from India to this country; to accumulate capital in India itself is practically impossible for the mass of the people.

Reference has already been made to the Punjab; and those who are not convinced by the foregoing pages as to the great and increasing poverty of India, and the miserable condition of the mass of the agricultural population under our rule, ought to refer to Mr. Dadabhai Naoroji's correspondence with the Government of India in relation to the total production of that great province, and the amount which is available for the support of the people. It is indisputable that the Punjab is one of the wealthiest provinces, and that it is, at this time, exporting large quantities of wheat to England. According to Mr. Dadabhai's calculation—and this gentleman is now a member of the Legislative Council of Bombay—the total value of the produce of the Punjab in the year 1876-77, just ten years ago, was, at 2*s.* the rupee, £35,330,000 for a population of 17,600,000, or £2 per head at the outside. A previous calculation made by the same able writer for 1867-8 gave a return of 49*s.* 5*d.* per head;—the probability being that the province had become impoverished to the extent of a con-

PUNJAB 1876-7.

Cost of absolute Necessaries of life of an agricultural labourer.

FOOD.

MAN.

Items.	Quantity per day.	Quantity for 1 year	Price for Re. 1.	Cost for 1 year.	Remarks.
	Seers.	Seers.	Seers.	Rs. As.	
Flour . . .	1	365	25	14 9	The price in the Report is 20 Seers for 1st sort; I have taken 25°/。 lower price for lower quality.
Rice . . .	¼	91	13	7 0	The price in the Report is 10 Seers for 1st sort; I take 30°/。 lower price for inferior quality.
Dal . . .	⅛	45	18	2 8	The price in the Report is 16 seers; I take it 12°/。 lower.
Salt . . .	1 oz.	11	9¼	1 3	The price of the Report—which is Government sale price.
Ghee . . .	1 ,,	11	3	3 11	The price in the Report is less than 2 seers. In taking 3 seers, I lower it above 50°/。, or rather to the price of oil. The quantity 1 oz. is also rather low for a Punjabee.
Condiment .	2 pies worth.			3 13	These are regarded as under the mark.
Tobacco . .	1½ ,, ,,			2 14	
Vegetables .	1 ,, ,,			1 8	
Total.				37 2	Without any meat, sugar, milk, or any drink or any kind of luxury whatever.

WOMAN.

All the above items will be nearly the same, except tobacco. Deducting tobacco it will be Rs. 34-2 as. Say Rs. 32.

2 MORE MEMBERS IN A FAMILY.

1 Young person say between 12 and 18—say Rs. 26—though there will not be so much difference.
1 Young person under 12—say Rs. 0—though this cannot be the case generally.

PUNJAB 1876-7.

Cost of absolute Necessaries of life of an Agricultural Labourer (*continued*).

CLOTHING FOR 1 YEAR.

Man.	Rs. a.	Woman.	Rs. a.	Remarks.
2 Dhotees	1 0	2 Pajamas	1 0	No holiday clothing, nor for occasions of joy and sorrow are reckoned.
2 Pairs, shoes	1 0	1 Gagra	2 0	
1 Turban	1 0	2 Chadars	1 8	
2 Bandis for warm and cold weather	1 8	4 Cholees	1 0	
2 Kamlees	4 0	Bangles	0 8	
1 Small piece of cloth for langootee, etc.	0 4	2 Pairs shoes	0 8	
1 Chadar	0 12	Hair dressing	0 3	
1 Pajama	0 12			
Total	10 4		6 11	

For 1 young person say Rs. 6, for the 2nd say nothing.

FAMILY EXPENSES IN COMMON.

	Rs. a.		Remarks
Cottage Rs. 60. Say Rs.	4 0	for 1 year.	Calculated on the lowest scale without any furniture—such as cots or mats, or stools or anything.
Repairs	3 0		
Cooking and other utensils.	3 8		
Fire wood ¼ anna per day.	5 11		
Lamp oil 1 oz. per day at 3 seers per Re. 1	3 12		
Total	19 15		

Taking 4 in the Family.

	Food.	Clothing.	Family expenses.	Total.
	Rs.	Rs. a.	Rs. a.	
Man	37	10 4		
Woman	32	6 11		
Youth (12 to 18)	26	6 0		
Child (under 12)	0	0 0		
	95	22 15	19 15	137 14—say Rs. 136

Which will be Rs. 34 per head per annum in a family of 4—against the production of Rs. 20 per annum at the outside.

No wedding, birth, and funeral expenses calculated, nor medical, educational, social, and religious wants, but simply the absolute necessaries for existence in ordinary health, at the lowest scale of cost and quantity.

The prices this year are the lowest during 10 years.

siderable portion of the additional 9*s.* 5*d.* a head in the interval.

At all events, after the very elaborate calculations of Mr. Dadabhai Naoroji, which remain wholly unshaken up to this moment, "it seems clearly established that the value of the production of one of the best provinces in India is twenty rupees, or £2 per head per annum at the outside," or £10 for a family of five. Neither Bombay, Madras, nor the North-West Provinces can show such high returns, in which not only all agricultural but all manufacturing and mining values are included. The attempt—I might fairly say the ridiculous attempt—made by Mr. F. C. Danvers ("D." of *Fraser's Magazine*) to upset Mr. Dadabhai's calculation strengthens the terrible effect of the foregoing tables. They give the cost of the absolute necessaries of life for agricultural labourers to keep them in good health and physical strength, and they were submitted before their publication to many authorities, native and European, who were capable of judging as to their truth.

Surely once more it is impossible to overlook the significance of these statements. They show that in ordinary times the population is yet more impoverished even than Dr. W. W. Hunter has been forced to admit. Thus reduced in physique by persistent underfeeding and underclothing, their cattle deteriorating alike in number and in quality, as is shown not only in the Punjab but throughout India, can we wonder that when a serious drought does come the people die off by millions? Anglo-Indians of the high official grades sneer of course at all native evidence, and deny the capacity of native accountants. though Hindoos and Parsees are masters of trade statistics and finance; they refuse also to admit that any of their own countrymen who approach these questions without a tinge of prejudice, such as they themselves naturally must have in favour of their own administration, can possibly form even the slightest conception of the truth; they actually denounce the ablest men in the official hierarchy, men directly engaged in the work of administration, such as Messrs. Geddes, Carpenter, Cunningham, Irwin, Sullivan, Connell, Harman, Buck, Robertson, Cotton, who, seeing the increasing misery around them, have had the courage and the self-sacrifice to risk all their professional prospects by telling the truth about the effects of our rule.

None the less, and in spite of public apathy or official prejudice, that truth must make way. Although the last number of the official blue-book, on "The Moral and Material Progress of India," has the assurance to state, in contradiction to every ascertained fact, that "a higher standard of comfort is gradually being recognised among the agricultural classes," no one for a moment believes any such thing. The gross unscrupulousness of official apologists in such matters I have already exposed in Chapter II.

I am not often able to agree with Mr. Robert Giffen, the head of the Statistical Department of the Board of Trade, who may indeed be considered a professional optimist in every sense, so when he says "that there is very little new and fertile soil to appropriate; there is no sign that land is being rapidly taken into cultivation," when he adds that there are "signs on the contrary of exhaustion in the agriculture and of an approach to limits of production according to the means at the disposal of the population. India for many years to come will be an increasingly dangerous problem for statesmen to deal with"—when Mr Giffen, I say, who a few years before held the directly opposite opinion, is forced to make such a gloomy forecast as this in a public address, those who, like myself, have never wearied of pointing to the facts, may well hope that ere long all will open their eyes. It is at any rate much too late in the day for Sir Juland Danvers to try to reassure his countrymen in the *Asiatic Quarterly Review* for April 1886, by the unsupported, and on the face of it absurd statement that "the food produce of India not only supplies her own wants, but is able to meet the demands of other countries"!

Figures again, official figures, are sadly against the officials themselves. Sir Juland Danvers gives them himself in the very article referred to. The total population of British India by the census of 1881 is put at 224,000,000. There are but 262,340,837 acres under any sort of cultivation in the same area, and of these no fewer than 113,345,991 acres are fallow. Thus but 148,991,846 acres are actually being cultivated for food, and other agricultural products, cotton, indigo, opium, etc., included; or 10,000,000 acres fewer than I have given and calculated upon in Chapter I. When 224,000,000 people have to be supported on the produce of 148,991,846 acres, millions of acres of which are necessarily devoted to non-edible crops, I do not think an observer needs the special skill of Sir James Caird to be able to say with certainty that the great majority of this population must be seriously underfed, and that tens of millions must be in the lowest depths of poverty compatible with human existence.

Look at this question of Indian famines from what point of view we will, still the increasing impoverishment and deterioration alike of men and cattle force themselves upon us as the conclusion to be drawn from all unbiassed testimony as well as from the *a priori* consideration of the figures furnished by the Government of India itself. Sir James Caird's solemn warning recurs again to the mind: "An exhausting agriculture and an increasing population must come to a deadlock. No reduction of the assessment can be more than a postponement of the inevitable catastrophe."

THE DRAIN OF PRODUCE.

The chief, indeed the paramount, reason for all this fearful impoverishment has been so often given in the preceding pages, that it is necessary to do little more than show that the drain of produce —the commercial tribute for which no return is given—has now attained to such a volume, that, if it goes on, economical bankruptcy, with an accompanying fearful social cataclysm, is inevitable within a comparatively short period. Sad to say, the hopeful spirit with which I began my studies in Indian finance and administration thirteen years ago has been wholly unjustified hitherto. The upper and middle classes at home are too deeply interested in the maintenance of the system to be willing, as classes, to admit the truth. They own the debt of India, their sons find a career in India, they flatter themselves with a sense of Imperial dignity and moral rectitude, at the same time that they fill their pockets from India. Five per cent. per annum cannot possibly be wrong, though millions must starve in order that it may be punctually paid; pensions must be met, though the natives have no voice in voting them; military and home charges must be maintained at their present high level, though they fall with crushing weight upon the poverty-stricken Indian ryots. The effect of this has already been seen reflected in the budgets of successive finance ministers as the growing loss by exchange, and, only too legibly, in the officially-recorded misery of the people of India.

Let us look closer. Taking the trade figures for the *ten* years 1875 to 1884 inclusive, in the same way that the trade figures for the *twenty* years 1857 to 1876 inclusive, were taken at p. 56, the grand total of Indian exports and imports amounts to £717,635,495 and £550,177,334 respectively, showing a difference of £167,458,101 Discriminating between merchandise and bullion in the imports of £550,177,334, we have merchandise imported in the ten years to the value of £442,589,727, and £107,587,607 of bullion. Between 1875 and 1884 the total export and import trade increased in round figures from £102,000,000 to £157,000,000, or a development of more than fifty per cent., after having doubled in the previous twenty years.

Once more, therefore, we are treated to the usual

stock commonplaces. Trade increased fifty per cent.! What better can you want? Exports still largely exceed imports; nothing can be more sound. Great inflow of bullion; that in itself settles the question!

But on the same principle as before fifteen per cent. must be added to the total valuation of exports, which is calculated at the Indian ports, in order to make allowance—on a very low scale be it observed—for freight, profit, and insurance. Consequently the value of the imports to balance these exports should be £717,635,495 plus fifteen per cent. on this amount, or £825,280,819. They were actually £550,177,334. Here is a discrepancy to start with of more than £275,000,000 in the ten years. Out of the actual imports, however, £107,587,607 represented bullion. Here again, applying the previous method, certainly not less than £60,000,000 of this represents import of treasure on loan, to say nothing of what may be imported for native States. It is, as I have said before, treasure which has been borrowed for a definite period, which is still owing, and which has to be repaid. This, therefore, is no genuine trade import. It is to be observed also that the proportion of treasure imported tends steadily to increase upon the average.

At any rate, on the old calculations, which have never yet been successfully impugned, and which really are much below rather than above the mark, we have here the original disparity of £275,000,000 plus £60,000,000, as the drain from India without any commercial return during the ten-year period 1875 to 1886. That amounts to no less a sum than £335,000,000, or at the rate of £33,500,000 a year!

This I say is still an understatement. But even as the figures stand, what does £33,500,000 of steady annual depletion represent from a population of 224,000,000 persons whose total gross produce is valued at no more than £400,000,000 by officials, and at £300,000,000, by able native statists; whose entire cultivated acreage, moreover, is, again using only official statistics, 148,000,000 acres? I say that such a state of things, such fearful impoverishment, has never before been heard of in all the long history of mankind.

But affairs, as the finance minister himself is forced to admit, are getting worse instead of better. They are indeed. He looks at the matter only from the financial point of view. Let us look at it from a higher standpoint. Owing to the fall of silver, less than 1*s.* 6*d.* now represents the value of the rupee. India is therefore obliged to remit to England, in order to make up the required amount of the sterling exchange, more than *one-third more produce than formerly* to meet the home charges, etc. Now consider the following official figures relative to the exports and imports of merchandise only for the year 1884-85.

Exports, £81,968,451.
Imports, £49,113,374.

Now add fifteen per cent. to the exports as before, for profits, etc., or £12,295,267, and we find that the imports ought to have been £93,263,738 in order merely to balance the exports. They were (exclusive of bullion) only, as we see, £49,113,374. This shows a disparity on that account of more than £44,000,000 against India on the merchandise account alone in that year! In the year 1885-86 matters have been still worse.

And yet in the face of these really appalling figures a man in the position of Sir Juland Danvers gravely asks us to congratulate ourselves upon the fact that the export of wheat from India has increased from 1,775,954 cwt. in 1874 to 21,001,412 cwt. in 1884. Is it reasonable to believe that, after the lucid expositions of the late Permanent Under-Secretary of State for India, Sir Louis Mallet, as to the inevitable results to the people of India of a drain less than half this amount, our Anglo-Indian officials can really be blind to the facts?

I put at the end of this section the official tables of exports and imports from the "Statistical Abstract," in order that my figures may be checked; and I repeat that the drain from India on English account represented an annual average of £33,500,000, for which no commercial return was given. This in addition to the large salaries paid to Europeans, military and civil, in India itself.

"But this drain must be stanched; taxation must be lowered; more natives must be employed; England, in short, must rise to the level of her great responsibilities, and take order with the ex-officials who pour forth optimist harangues in praise of their own administrative capacity. With one accord Sir James Caird, Mr. Buck, Mr. Harman, and Mr Robertson, all skilled agriculturists, declare that the soil of India is undergoing steady and permanent deterioration. Mr. Robertson puts the deterioration in Coimbatore at thirty per cent. in thirty years, and points out how the natives are driven to grow cotton for sale instead of food to eat, and literally to starve themselves in order to pay the Government assessment owing to this deterioration. Thirty per cent. less produce per acre in thirty years!

"Who can wonder? The produce is taken away to be brought over here to an increasing extent, and there is now less manure than ever to put back into the soil. At the same time the destruction of the forests for railway sleepers and fuel has, as in the United States and Australia, most seriously affected the climate for the worse. Drought and floods alternate in districts where formerly the rainfall was beneficial and equable. Such is our foresight in India, such the care of our civilisation of to-day for the civilisation of the human beings of to-morrow.

"From all the provinces comes the same sad cry. From the North-West and from Oudh, from Bombay as well as from Madras, from large tracts of Bengal, and even from the Punjab, one mournful story is heard: the land does not, as of old, bring forth of its abundance; there is no blessing on the crops in our day. A deteriorated race of men, an inferior description of bullocks, bear witness to the truth of what they say. By the side of this drain and the consequent impoverishment of the soil, helped on by denudation, all the rest of our blunders, great as they have been, are mere child's play.

"Thus on every side the prospect is gloomy and overcast, and in the opinion of the ablest observers we are drawing nearer and nearer to an almost overwhelming disaster. Year after year we take from India agricultural produce which she cannot spare, because we are masters of the country, and, paying ourselves handsomely all round, leave those who depend upon us for safety to perish from want. Whilst we are disputing about the defence of the empire we ourselves are preparing its ruin, only to learn the truth too late; the knocking will come through the darkness, from without, the murder within will be done."*

* "England for All," p. 144, "India." The chapter from which this extract from a little book of mine with this title is taken, was translated and distributed in many of the native languages.

TOTAL VALUE of MERCHANDISE and TREASURE respectively IMPORTED into and EXPORTED from BRITISH INDIA, by SEA, from and to FOREIGN COUNTRIES, including GOVERNMENT STORES and TREASURE, in each of the under-mentioned Official Years.

OFFICIAL YEARS ended 31st March.	IMPORTS.			EXPORTS.		
	Merchandise.	Treasure.	Total.	Merchandise.	Treasure.	Total.
	£	£	£	£	£	£
1875 . . .	36,222,113	8,141,047	44,363,160	56,359,240	1,625,309	57,984,549
1876 . . .	38,891,656	5,300,722	44,192,378	58,091,495	2,200,236	60,291,731
1877 . . .	37,440,631	11,436,120	48,876,751	61,013,891	4,029,898	65,043,789
1878 . . .	41,464,185	17,355,459	58,819,644	65,222,328	2,210,996	67,433,324
1879 . . .	37,800,594	7,056,749	44,857,343	60,937,513	3,982,228	64,919,741
1880 . . .	41,166,003	11,655,395	52,821,398	67,212,363	2,035,148	69,247,511
1881 . . .	53,116,770	8,988,214	62,104,984	74,580,602	1,440,441	76,021,043
1882 . . .	49,113,374	11,322,781	60,436,155	81,968,451	1,099,747	83,068,198
1883 . . .	52,095,711	13,453,157	65,548,868	83,485,123	1,042,059	84,527,182
1884 . . .	55,278,690	12,877,963	68,156,653	88,089,933	1,008,494	89,098,427
Total for the 10 years	442,589,727	107,587,607	550,177,334	696,960,939	20,674,556	717,635,495

TOTAL VALUE of MERCHANDISE and TREASURE respectively IMPORTED into and EXPORTED from BRITISH INDIA, by SEA, from and to FOREIGN COUNTRIES on PRIVATE ACCOUNT, excluding GOVERNMENT STORES and TREASURE, in each of the under-mentioned Official Years.

OFFICIAL YEARS ended 31st March.	IMPORTS.			EXPORTS.		
	Merchandise.	Treasure.	Total.	Merchandise.	Treasure.	Total.
	£	£	£	£	£	£
1875	34,645,262	8,141,047	42,786,309	56,312,261	1,592,721	57,904,982
1876	37,112,668	5,300,722	42,413,390	58,045,405	2,115,144	60,160,549
1877	35,367,177	11,436,118	46,803,295	60,961,632	3,942,580	64,904,212
1878	39,326,003	17,355,459	56,681,462	65,185,713	2,155,136	67,340,849
1879	36,566,194	7,056,749	43,622,943	60,893,611	3,895,545	64,789,156
1880	39,742,166	11,655,395	51,397,561	67,173,158	1,928,828	69,101,986
1881	50,308,834	8,988,214	59,297,048	74,531,282	1,409,403	75,940,685
1882	46,992,084	11,322,781	58,314,865	81,901,960	1,097,387	82,999,347
1883	50,003,041	13,453,157	63,466,198	83,400,865	980,859	84,381,724
1884	52,703,233	12,877,963	65,581,196	88,035,139	979,759	89,014,898
Total for the 10 years	422,766,662	107,587,605	530,354,267	696,441,026	20,097,362	716,538,388

TOTAL NET VALUE of MERCHANDISE and TREASURE (excluding Government Stores and Treasure) IMPORTED into and EXPORTED from BRITISH INDIA by SEA, from and to FOREIGN COUNTRIES on PRIVATE ACCOUNT, in each of the under-mentioned Years.

YEARS ended 31 March.	Merchandise.		Net Exports of Merchandise.	Treasure.		Net Imports of Treasure.	Surplus Exports of Merchandise.
	Imported.	Exported.		Imported.	Exported.		
	£	£	£	£	£	£	£
1867 (11 Months)	29,014,741	41,859,994	12,845,253	13,229,533	1,950,435	11,279,098	1,566,155
1868	35,664,320	50,874,001	15,209,681	11,775,374	1,025,336	10,750,038	4,459,643
1869	35,931,374	53,062,165	17,130,791	14,366,588	776,082	13,590,506	3,540,285
1870	32,879,643	52,471,376	19,591,733	13,954,807	1,025,386	12,929,421	6,662,312
1871	33,348,246	55,331,825	21,983,579	5,444,823	1,587,180	3,857,643	18,125,936
1872	30,810,776	63,185,848	32,375,072	11,573,813	1,421,173	10,152,640	22,222,432
1873	30,473,069	55,236,295	24,763,226	4,556,585	1,273,979	3,282,606	21,480,620
1874	31,628,497	54,960,786	23,332,289	5,792,534	1,879,071	3,913,463	19,418,826
1875	34,645,262	56,312,261	21,666,999	8,141,047	1,592,721	6,548,326	15,118,673
1876	37,112,668	58,045,405	20,932,737	5,300,722	2,115,144	3,185,578	17,747,159
1877	35,367,177	60,961,632	25,594,455	11,436,118	3,942,580	7,493,538	18,100,917
1878	39,326,003	65,185,713	25,859,710	17,355,459	2,155,136	15,200,323	10,659,387
1879	36,566,194	60,893,611	24,327,417	7,056,749	3,895,545	3,161,204	21,166,213
1880	39,742,166	67,173,158	27,430,992	11,655,395	1,928,828	9,726,567	17,704,425
1881	50,308,834	74,531,282	24,222,448	8,988,214	1,409,403	7,578,811	16,643,637
1882	46,992,084	81,901,960	34,909,876	11,322,781	1,097,387	10,225,394	24,684,482
1883	50,003,041	83,400,865	33,397,824	13,453,157	980,859	12,472,298	20,925,526
1884	52,703,233	88,035,139	35,331,906	12,877,963	979,759	11,898,204	23,433,702
Total for the 18 Years	682,517,328	1,123,423,316	440,905,988	188,281,662	31,036,004	157,245,658	283,660,330

PUBLIC WORKS.

After the foregoing complete exposition of India's dire poverty, any elaborate examination of our expenditure on Public Works is really unnecessary. It is true that the Brothers Strachey published four years ago a large octavo volume proving to their own satisfaction, and that presumably of the other officials who are largely responsible for the present deplorable state of things, that the Finances and the Public Works of India have been admirably managed by themselves. But we may look in vain through their pages for any effective answer to the contentions even of the Committee of the House of Commons on Indian Public Works. When also we find it stated at the end of the volume that "there has been no attempt made to support the assertion by fact," that borrowing for such works is "ruinous or mischievous," and that "viewed financially, and in the interests of India itself, the charge for the debt is not serious," it is permissible to throw on one side such prejudiced evidence altogether, especially when we remember that Sir John Strachey, as Finance Minister, himself pointed out the serious drain upon India involved by the Home Charges.

No one who has ever devoted much attention to Indian affairs can doubt that wells, tanks, and carefully-planned irrigation works on a large scale have been and are beneficial to the country. It is unfortunately beyond question that we greatly neglected these matters during the early years of our supremacy ; it is also true that some of our more important enterprises have been costly failures. But a good native or English administrator would find plenty to do in this direction in all parts of India if only the means were at hand. There are 40,000 broached tanks in the Deccan alone, and the need for more wells has been insisted upon by all observers. The example of what was done in Travancore is ever before us to show what extraordinary results can be produced in favourable circumstances. But to borrow out of the country, even for good irrigation works, is a dangerous process ; nor on this point need anything be added to the excellent remarks of Lord Salisbury already quoted. If the Tory statesman had had the courage of his opinions, we should not have been landed in our present perilous position. If, too, the millions which we take from India were devoted to useful waterworks and tree-planting, things would soon be very different. As it is, according to Sir Juland Danvers, a net return of £1,130,759 was obtained on an expenditure of £25,586,807 on irrigation works. But it should be remembered that much of the water is forced upon the people, and that when allowance is made for the great success of Sir Arthur Cotton's schemes in Madras, this is no very great return ; further, that the interest, after all, is paid out of the country.

But the blunders made in relation to irrigation works are as nothing, beside what has been in respect to railways. A total sum of £155,500,000 was spent or guaranteed up to the year 1884 in the following proportions :—

Lines Guaranteed	£105,300,000
State Lines	43,000,000
Native States	3,800,000
British Companies	3,400,000
	£155,500,000

Owing to the cheaper construction of the State lines the average cost per mile has been reduced from £21,000 a mile to £13,000 a mile, and there were 12,330 miles open last year. The gross return is £16,066,225, and the net, after deducting £8,156,157 for working expenses, say £8,000,000, in round figures.

Now it is very difficult for Englishmen whose railroads were the natural growth from their industrial system, and were built with their own capital, to understand that these railways in a poor country like India—224,000,000 people subsisting on the produce of 148,000,000 acres of land—represent little more than huge syphons, which facilitate the impoverishment of the country. But so it is. Railways do not produce wealth in themselves; they simply save time and cost of transport, thus enabling carriers, etc., to turn to other occupations. But when the profits of these railways are deducted even in famine years and brought over here, all benefit is gone, and an enormous, I had nearly said an incalculable, injury is inflicted on the people. Thus when it is soberly contended by Sir Juland Danvers that the guaranteed railways have given £5,000,000 to the railway servants in wages and £5,000,000 to the shareholders, I am entitled to ask for evidence of the increased wealth thus distributed. There is, as I have shown, no such increase of wealth, but great and increasing poverty for which the railways and the manner in which they were built are largely the cause. India pays England a rent of £8,000,000 to absentee shareholders for the use of the railways, besides the heavy salaries to Europeans. I challenge any Anglo-Indian official to show that this is an advantageous arrangement for India.

It seems, however, that no further attention is to be paid to the recommendations of the Committee of the House of Commons, of which the late Mr. Henry Fawcett was a member, that the Public Works Department—corrupt, unscrupulous, and jobbing as it has been proved to be—is allowed full control, and that the extravagant and pernicious system of guarantees, which even Sir John Strachey and General Richard Strachey protest against, is to be reintroduced.

CONCLUSION.

I have written to very little purpose if I have not by this time convinced all unprejudiced readers that the present state of our Indian Empire is so dangerous, that it is the bounden duty of Englishmen of all classes to look carefully into the facts. It is impossible to push aside Lord Lawrence, Lord Canning, Lord Ripon, Sir James Caird, Mr. James Geddes, Mr. Robertson, etc., as so many ignorant or prejudiced persons. Yet all of them have given it as their opinion that India is a very poor country, and that we ought greatly to increase the employment of natives as well as to practise the most relentless economy in every department. Instead of this, the process of Europeanisation goes steadily on, economy is opposed by the whole official class, the drain of produce yearly swells in volume, and the army is to be increased.

What is the remedy? There is manifestly no remedy which the governing classes of the United Kingdom—Irishmen have their full share in the impoverishment of India—are ready to accept. In vain do men point to the admirable administration of Baroda, Travancore, Jeypore, Hyderabad, under Native Government lightly controlled by English supervision; in vain do Finance Ministers cry out against the financial effects of the home charges, and economists inveigh against the fearful capitalist absenteeism. All preach to deaf ears. Those who know the truth dare not face it, but, fearing the pressure of officialism, and feeling public opinion as represented by the press too strong for them, console themselves by saying, "It will last our time." Indian loans are taken up here, and even on the Continent, as if no end would ever come to these good times, and that India could sustain this terrible economical misrule for another generation.

I appeal, then, on this matter away from those who are interested in maintaining the present harmful and ruinous domination in India to the working classes of my countrymen, who are now the real masters of India, to say whether they are content that such ruin should be wrought in their name; whether, for the sake of the interest, pensions, and profits of the non-producing minority of Englishmen, they intend that 224,000,000 of people should be slowly bled to death; whether, in the name of a bastard Imperialism, they will consent to the continuance of a system which will be worthily coupled with the hideous tyranny of the Spaniards in Mexico and South America?

There is no time to be lost. If a peaceable settlement is to be made it must be made at once. Let us not deceive ourselves. From one end to the other of the great Peninsula, where a mere handful of Europeans keep more than 270,000,000 of people directly or indirectly under control, the word is passing, with all the secret celerity of the East, that this misery can be no longer endured, that the day is coming for agitation and for action. I know whereof I write. It is not in London alone that the bankruptcy of India is being discussed; it is not only in St. Petersburg that our military strength is known to a man. The approach of Russia to our frontier is a danger doubtless; but our greatest, by far our greatest, danger in India is within our own border. If the agricultural population, or any considerable proportion of it, should become disaffected, not all the resources of the empire could retain possession of the country. There are not wanting symptoms that dangerous disaffection has already begun.

But does not justice demand that we should act? Is it right that we should continue our present system? To those two questions I say there is but one possible answer.

A stern and immediate reduction of the Indian drain by at least one-half—no matter what shriek of "confiscation" may be raised; a deliberate reconstruction of native governments wherever possible; a steady but rapid substitution of natives for Europeans in all our departments, might yet save us from overwhelming disaster, which could not but be reflected in yet worse misery and starvation than great masses of our population are already suffering from at home. But to carry out these indispensable reforms calls for a relentless determination, which no man and no body of men in England has yet shown. A strong and compact phalanx of Anglo-Indians, official and non-official, backed by the great bulk of the interest-receiving and profit-making class, resolutely oppose all change. The fate of Lord Ripon has daunted others, and all fear the charges of want of patriotism or meaner imputations which those who are pecuniarily interested in keeping up the existing injustice never hesitate to make. Therefore it is that upright men in every class should band themselves together, and endeavour to awaken the mass of Englishmen to their duty in this matter. The future alike of India and of England is in the balance, and he is indeed worse than a coward who, at the risk of calumny and misrepresentation, dare not stand up for the truth and champion the welfare of 220,000,000 of people who as yet have no effective voice in the management of their own affairs.

V.

THE SILVER QUESTION.

For some years past the continuous fall in the value of silver has given rise to a great deal of discussion, and things have now come to such a pass—silver being worth, and that only nominally, 43*d.* an ounce, and the rupee worth only 1*s.* 4½*d.*—that a serious agitation is being carried on, alike in the United States and in Europe, with a view to restoring, if possible, silver to its old position with relation to gold. Unfortunately the subject, in itself one not at first sight likely to generate heat, has been treated with so much warmth that it is difficult to separate mere prejudice from argument. The so-called bi-metallists, who wish to maintain a permanent relation between gold and silver of 1 to 15½, denounce the monometallists, who wish to leave things as they are, as bigots and fetish worshippers. The monometallists, on the other hand, treat the bimetallists, though these number in their ranks some of the ablest practical men of business in the world, with the most galling contempt. Thus a truly theological rancour has been stirred up between the contending parties, and the real issues are obscured by a cloud of strong and irritating language.

As I have not the least feeling on the question, and hitherto have taken no part whatever in the discussion; as, farther, I am not engaged in mercantile business, and have no interest which is affected in any way by the price of silver or the rate of the Indian exchanges, I may at least claim that I approach the matter without any prejudice. And, in the first place, I cannot but observe that it is the tendency of those who advocate the "rehabilitation" of silver to attribute too much importance to the fall in the value of silver as affecting prices, as well as in producing trade depression. A simple instance will show what I mean. At all periods of crisis and industrial stagnation,—and we have had no fewer than seven such crises in the present century,—prices invariably fall heavily as compared with what they were during the years of trade prosperity immediately preceding the collapse. Now 1857, the year of the fourth crisis of the century, was also perhaps the year when gold was more plentiful, with respect to the demand for it for currency purposes, than it has ever been in the history of the two metals. The gold discoveries of California, Australia, and New Zealand took place from 1849 to 1852; the returns from the Russian mines were going on at the same time, and so large was the output of gold up to 1857 from all quarters, so little labour did it take to produce it as compared with what was formerly the case, that positively Cobden, Chevallier, Jevons, and others were engaged in calculating what effect a permanent reduction in the value of gold, and consequently a permanently high level of prices, would have upon all civilised countries. The demonetisation of gold was actually discussed. The danger, then, was a depreciation of gold, as now it is said to be its appreciation; the asserted drawback then was a range of high prices, the alleged drawback now is a low range of prices. Yet in 1857, and again in 1866, —periods when the supply of gold was even in excess of the demand for currency purposes,—prices of produce fell, owing to causes entirely outside of the mere mechanical operations of currency.

Thus a fall of prices may occur when the supply of gold is rising, as in 1857 and 1866; and it may occur when the supply of gold is falling, as in 1875 and 1883. Or, which is merely a repetition of the same thing, a heavy fall of prices may occur when the supply of silver is falling or stationary, and its relative value is high, as in 1857 and 1866; and it may occur when the supply of silver is rising and its relative value is low, as in 1875 and 1883. True, the fall was not nearly *so* heavy; but fall there was.

Again, the heavy fall in the Indian exchange has been contemporaneous with a vast increase in the payments made by India to this country without any commercial return. These payments are represented in England by bills drawn by the Indian Council upon India in rupees. These bills, which are, of course, virtually so much remittance thrown upon the market for sale, entirely upset all the ordinary course of dealings in silver or in rupees,—the silver currency of India. The exchange falls more and more, not altogether because merely of the greater supply or the cheaper production of silver itself, but because in the circumstances, the growing indebtedness of India must make the exchange more and more unfavourable. Thus her export trade is unduly fostered, at the same time that the drain of produce to this country is greatly increased. As one result the people of India have to export to this country more than one-third more produce than is represented by the nominal value of their yearly indebtedness in sovereigns; and the rupee remaining, as it seems, unchanged in purchasing power in the interior of the country, Indian goods and produce can be sold at inordinately cheap rates on this market. The cry concerning the fall in silver, therefore, arises from three quarters: from the Government of India, which has to incur a manifest loss on remittance amounting now to fully £6,000,000 in the year; from those of the Anglo-Indian employés and pensioners—a very powerful body,—who have to make their remittances or receive their pensions on a silver basis; and from our wheat growers and others who find that, owing partly to the fall of silver some 25 or 30 per cent., they are undersold, with no prospect of being able to meet the competition. Neither can it be denied that an unstable exchange, fluctuating between wide limits, but ever tending downwards, does introduce too much of the speculative element into all the relations of business. But the fearful indebtedness of India to England would occasion increasing disturbance, even if silver had never been demonetised in Germany, and the great silver-lead and silver mines of the United States and Mexico had not reduced the cost of production so largely. The fact that the depreciation of the rupee on the markets of the world has not been accompanied by a falling-off in its purchasing power in India itself, but that it actually purchases more now than it did ten years ago, introduces also a most perturbing element into all the theories of a self-adjusting currency. The effect in stimulating Indian exports, or exports from any silver-using country where the purchasing power of the depreciated currency is still maintained, is seen at once. A sovereign to-day will buy more than 14½ rupees, the par exchange being 10 rupees. These 14½ rupees will, however, purchase as much produce *in India* as if the exchange were still at par. It is easy to see, therefore, why Asiatic produce can be sold cheap; and similar instances are given with reference to Chili and other countries in the July number of the *City Quarterly Magazine.* The exchange being low in these countries, they are able, in certain commodities, to undersell other countries where the exchange is maintained at par, and there is no heavy external indebtedness.

Nevertheless, when full account is taken of international crises, which are longer and more severe at each recurrence, as bringing about a fall in prices, due to causes which need not be examined here; when allowance is made for the terrible effect of the Indian indebtedness upon which Mr. A. J. Wilson, I am glad to see, has again enlarged of late, there remain certain mechanical difficulties which Mr. Robert Giffen, Mr. Arthur Crump, and Mr. A. J. Wilson, on their side, do not give sufficient weight to.

Everybody who knows anything at all about the subject must be well aware that no international agreement of any sort will make gold bullion, which it would cost say a thousand days' average labour to reproduce, exchange on the market of the world on an equality with silver bullion which it would take but seven hundred and fifty days' average labour to reproduce. As well might an enactment be made that ten yards of cotton should be always equal in value to ten yards of the finest Brussels lace all the world over. Neither is it possible to have two standards of value in the same country. Gold and silver being practically the only two precious metals, one or the other, uncoined, must be a commodity in relation to its fellow, both, of course, owing their value to the fact that they are socially useful, and that it requires human labour to produce them. When so produced, they represent a concrete embodiment of social human labour in which other embodiments of useful social human labour are estimated or priced. But inasmuch as they vary in value with reference to one another in proportion to their cost of production (or fluctuate with the supply at any given moment), they cannot both be general standards of value at the same time. This has been pointed out by every economist who has ever written. Furthermore, there is little evidence that Europe needs more currency, in view of the great economy in the use of the precious metals which has been introduced of late years by the use of bills, cheques, the establishment of clearing-houses, etc. An increase of currency beyond what is needed to facilitate the circulation of commodities is simply useless; and if a universal rise of prices is to be brought about, it has been vehemently urged that what takes place is merely a nominal change, in so far as it is not due to greater commercial activity. The effect of the present general low range of prices for commodities, including silver, and the appreciation of gold, is that all State debt and mortgage holders, all persons with fixed incomes paid in gold, are better off than they were at the time when there was talk of demonetising gold by reason of its depreciation; and those who are producing on the old level are doing so at a diminished profit, or even at a loss. This is no doubt important; though it concerns chiefly the division of profits when made. But, seeing that commodities are really exchanged against commodities, the action of money being merely a superficial phenomenon, the low range of prices cannot in the long run affect business as business. Exporters and importers will adjust themselves to that as to other changes. The difficulty comes in, as already remarked, when silver coins which in the market of the world are worth but two-thirds of their par value still remain, in the country where they are used, of the same exchange value for commodities that they had prior to that depreciation. That the extraordinary development of machinery of late years in all departments has had a great deal to do with the general fall in prices, measured in gold, is also undoubted, and in nothing is this more displayed than in iron, where Asiatic competition is, so far, practically non-existent. But in the matter of competition in goods of the like character, the truth that silver-using countries can undersell is manifest, though it is also clear that they do so in the long run to their own great disadvantage and at a ruinous sacrifice of their future.

While, therefore, it is foolish to overlook the economical causes which are independent of the relations between the precious metals; to imagine that the "depression of trade," which has been a hard reality enough to the working classes, whatever the floundering Royal Commission may say, is chiefly due to the depreciation of silver; or to declare, with one ardent bi-metallist, that the theory of cycles in trade is exploded; it would, at the same time, be as foolish to ignore the fact that great disturbance, and in some cases great hardship, to large classes of people has been caused by this fall in prices. Furthermore, no one can surely allege that the currency of the world cannot be improved; that the demonetisation of silver has not produced a great effect already; or even that international and legal arrangements cannot make a far larger quantity of silver available for currency purposes, without depreciation, than is the case now, presuming this step to be desirable on other grounds. The advocates of monometallism are too apt to treat the whole subject as if no arguments on the other side had been adduced at all.

Now, it is an undoubted fact that some 900,000,000 people on this planet still use a silver currency exclusively, and their trade is increasingly important. It is also not disputed that France had a double currency maintained at 15½ to 1 proportion. In addition it is not denied that the present excessive depreciation of the inferior metal began with the demonetisation of silver by Germany in 1872, followed by the cessation of the coinage of silver for legal tender by France in 1874. This has thrown an ever-increasing amount of the output of silver, which itself has increased largely, upon the market, while the output of gold has greatly diminished. Now, too, it is becoming uncertain whether the United States will continue to coin unlimited quantities of silver, which necessarily reduces its price still lower. In short, it is impossible to say to what price silver will not fall if so-called natural causes are left to work their will. Such continuous depreciation will eventually have the effect of limiting the quantity mined; but since there is little likelihood of any cheaper gold supply, there will always be a danger in this direction. The monometallists also ought to state how it is that silver has only fallen so greatly since its demonetisation by Germany, if the fall is not largely due to that cause. India was *very* heavily indebted before 1874, yet the exchange value of the rupee was maintained. Why should not Germany remonetise silver? And if Germany, why should not we remonetise silver by an international agreement with reference to dollars and half-dollars? An international silver and gold coinage would be a great convenience, though, as already stated, no international agreement can by any possibility make gold and silver bullion sell at a lower or higher scale with reference to each other than their relative cost of production justified. Yet, why should not a full dollar and half dollar, equal to two rupees and a rupee, as Mr. Seyd proposed, be made current coin at a specific ratio throughout Europe, the United States, England, and India? None of the evils foreshadowed by the monometallists could be worse than the present general uncertainty, which is becoming a serious stumbling-block, and is, as has already been shown, increasingly ruinous to India. Anything which will even temporarily reduce the drain of produce from that country would be highly beneficial from every point of view. Though the present depreciation might right itself in the long run,—and merchants need not care, in dealing with commodities whether the exchange be high or low, seeing that they make all their calculations accordingly,—it is a most terrible thing for India that she should have, as already shown on page 158, to transmit on account of her home charges over one-third more—or, at 1*s.* 4*d.* the rupee, one-half more—produce to this country than would be the case if the rupee were maintained at or near par.

The two following tables are taken from Mr. Ernest Seyd's pamphlet. The first is taken from Dr. Soetbeer:—

		Kilos. Gold.	Kilos. Silver.	Percentage Gold.	Percentage Silver.
Average in periods of five years.	1851—1855	197,515	888,115	18·2	81·8
	1856—1860	206,058	904,990	18·5	81·5
	1861—1865	185,123	1,101,150	14·4	85·6
	1866—1870	191,900	1,339,085	12·5	87·5
	1871—1875	170,675	1,969,425	8·0	92·0
	1876—1880	172,800	2,450,252	6·6	93·4
	1881	157,900	2,592,639	5·7	94·3
	1882	146,900	2,769,065	5·0	95·0
	1883	143,940	2,895,520	4·7	95·3
	1884	140,000	2,860,000	4·7	95·3
	1885			4·2	95·8

Average for five years.	Gold per cent. weight.	Silver per cent. weight.		Highest.	Lowest.	Average Dr. Soetbeer.	
1851 to 1855	18·2	81·8	1851	$61\frac{5}{8}$	60	61	Discoveries of gold in California and Australia.
			1852	$61\frac{7}{8}$	$59\frac{7}{8}$	$60\frac{1}{2}$	
			1853	$62\frac{3}{8}$	$60\frac{5}{8}$	$61\frac{1}{2}$	
			1854	$61\frac{7}{8}$	$60\frac{7}{8}$	$61\frac{1}{2}$	
			1855	$61\frac{5}{8}$	60	$61\frac{5}{16}$	
1856 to 1860	18·5	81·5	1856	$62\frac{1}{4}$	$60\frac{1}{2}$	$61\frac{5}{16}$	Period during which the largest amount of gold was produced.
			1857	$62\frac{3}{8}$	61	$61\frac{3}{4}$	
			1858	$61\frac{7}{8}$	$60\frac{3}{4}$	$61\frac{5}{16}$	
			1859	$62\frac{3}{4}$	$61\frac{3}{4}$	$62\frac{1}{16}$	
			1860	$62\frac{3}{8}$	$61\frac{1}{4}$	$61\frac{11}{16}$	
1861 to 1865	14·4	85·6	1861	$61\frac{3}{4}$	$60\frac{1}{8}$	$60\frac{13}{16}$	Gold production falling off.
			1862	$62\frac{1}{8}$	61	$61\frac{7}{16}$	
			1863	$61\frac{3}{4}$	61	$61\frac{3}{8}$	
			1864	$62\frac{1}{2}$	$60\frac{5}{8}$	$61\frac{3}{8}$	
			1865	$61\frac{7}{8}$	$60\frac{1}{2}$	$61\frac{1}{16}$	
1866 to 1870	12·5	87·5	1866	$62\frac{1}{4}$	$60\frac{3}{8}$	$61\frac{1}{8}$	
			1867	$61\frac{1}{4}$	$60\frac{5}{16}$	$61\frac{9}{16}$	
			1868	$61\frac{1}{8}$	$60\frac{1}{8}$	$60\frac{1}{2}$	
			1869	61	60	$60\frac{7}{16}$	
			1870	62	$60\frac{1}{4}$	$60\frac{9}{16}$	
1871 to 1875	8·0	92·0	1871	$60\frac{7}{8}$	$60\frac{3}{16}$	$60\frac{1}{2}$	Demonetisation by Germany.
			1872	$61\frac{1}{8}$	$59\frac{1}{4}$	$60\frac{5}{16}$	
			1873	$59\frac{15}{16}$	$57\frac{7}{8}$	$59\frac{1}{4}$	
			1874	$59\frac{1}{2}$	$57\frac{1}{4}$	$58\frac{5}{16}$	
			1875	$57\frac{5}{8}$	$55\frac{1}{2}$	$56\frac{7}{8}$	
1876 to 1880	6·6	93·4	1876	$58\frac{1}{2}$	$46\frac{3}{4}$	$52\frac{3}{4}$	Panic in silver in July, and quick recovery.
			1877	$58\frac{1}{4}$	$53\frac{1}{4}$	$54\frac{13}{16}$	
			1878	$55\frac{1}{4}$	$49\frac{1}{2}$	$52\frac{9}{16}$	
			1879	$53\frac{3}{4}$	$48\frac{7}{8}$	$51\frac{1}{4}$	
			1880	$52\frac{7}{8}$	$51\frac{5}{8}$	$52\frac{1}{4}$	
For the year							
1881	5·7	94·3	...	$52\frac{7}{8}$	$50\frac{7}{8}$	$51\frac{11}{16}$	
1882	5·0	95·0	...	$52\frac{7}{16}$	50	$51\frac{5}{8}$	
1883	4·7	95·3	...	$52\frac{1}{16}$	50	$50\frac{9}{16}$	
1884	4·7	95·3	...	$51\frac{3}{8}$	$50\frac{5}{16}$	$50\frac{5}{8}$	
1885	4·2	95·8	...	50	$46\frac{7}{8}$	$48\frac{5}{8}$	

These tables have the merit of putting the facts with regard to gold and silver production clearly before us, though the price of silver at the time of writing, 43*d.*, is lower by far than any point yet reached. It will be seen, however, that, whereas the production of silver has increased more than threefold since 1851, the production of gold has decreased nearly one-third ; that, moreover, the disparity between the two productions is going on in a heightened ratio, though the price of silver to-day is but 43*d.*, as against 60*d.* to 61*d.* up to the date of the demonetisation of silver by Germany in 1872. It is certainly not a little remarkable as telling against the contentions of the monometallists, that, notwithstanding the great change between the relative amounts of gold and silver produced which had taken place from 1851 to 1874, varying from 18·2 per cent. of gold and 81.8 per cent. of silver in 1851-55 to 8 per cent. of gold and 92 per cent. of silver in 1874, the price of the inferior metal underwent no serious depreciation. This, although, as before remarked, the drain from India was even then not less than £20,000,000 a year, according to the admission of Sir John Strachey, and the standard of the rupee has remained unchanged.

Without, therefore, attempting to lay down the law upon this subject, it may at least be said that it is highly desirable, for the sake of our great dependency, that silver should be remonetised ; that it has never been conclusively shown that silver could not be remonetised ; that until it was demonetised by Germany the fall in its value was comparatively trifling ; and had this not been done it might possibly—in spite of greatly increased output—have remained comparatively trifling up to the present time. Here, as in other departments of business, is an opportunity for international inquiry; though that any amount of international agreement will prevent periods of terrible stagnation of trade, so long as the producers themselves have no control over production and exchange, I do not for one moment believe.

Recently the Government of India, driven to despair by the fact that all its small economies, as well as the proceeds of additional taxation and the amounts drawn from the provincial exchequers, threatened to be completely absorbed by the fall in the exchange, appointed Mr. O'Connor to inquire into the effects of this fall in the value of silver upon India and Indian producers. Necessarily, he reports that this fall is most injurious to India in every way, seeing that, in consequence of the fall in silver, not only, as has been so often repeated, is India obliged to remit to this country many millions more tons of agricultural produce in order to make up the amount of the drain for home payments in gold, but the agriculturists, in their ordinary dealings, are receiving a depreciated currency for their own produce, though this currency passes at the old level in India itself. Mr. O'Connor therefore enforces the arguments of Sir Auckland Colvin, the present Finance Minister, as to the great injury which India is suffering from this depreciation.

The only wonder is that sane men could be found to argue that India could by any possibility be benefited by the fall in silver. To begin with, all the enormous amount of that metal now in India is of less value relatively to all other commodities than it was in the markets of the world; and, sooner or later, this disparity must make itself felt. In addition, how can it be reasonably argued that the ryots gain by giving more of their produce for a less monetary return, if we stop at the first process of their disposal of their crop? As so often happens in these days of middle-class economy and superficial discussion, men's minds are completely confused by the merest absurdities. It is said, for example, that anything which tends to encourage exports is beneficial to India, because trade is thereby improved. Is it then beneficial to starving ryots that wheat or rice, which would feed them, should, to the amount of millions of tons, be shipped off to this country, because otherwise they could not make their payments or meet their assessments? Manifestly not. Yet that such increased export is beneficial is the silly sort of argument which the Government of India has been obliged to answer through Mr. O'Connor.

Beyond all question the fall in silver is most harmful to India and its people at this time, and the plainest common-sense would recognise that at once, if the old ideas did not obscure the fact that additional food is being sent out of the country for nothing. The danger now is, in regard to India, that this silver depreciation, which, though serious, is, after all, by no means the most serious difficulty at the present time, may blind people to the real causes of Indian poverty.

The pressure being brought to bear from India in favour of the remonetisation of silver, supported as it is by influential classes at home, is now backed up from America and Germany. In America Mr. Evarts, the Secretary for Foreign Affairs in the Republican administration, has brought the matter forward ; and the "silver ring," which has its agents on this side of the Atlantic, is constantly urging the question upon the public outside the House of Assembly and the Senate. Here in England it is said that Lord Randolph Churchill, the new Tory Chancellor of the Exchequer, is inclined to propose the appointment of a Royal Commission to examine into the whole matter ; an influential memorial has also been presented to Lord Salisbury on the subject ; and Mr. Goschen has declared that much of the present depression is due to the appreciation of gold. All are agreed, in fact, that nothing can be done unless England moves. If England and her colonies, including India, concert a common line of action with the United States and Germany, then the countries forming the so-called Latin Union—France, Italy, and Belgium—will gladly come in, and establish a definite international agreement which would influence the whole civilsed world. Such is the contention. England, then, being the principal commercial country, and virtually the commercial clearing-house of the world, and holding, therefore, the key to the currency position, it is necessary to examine briefly how the appreciation of gold, which we can all see is increasing rapidly on the average, if we look at the prices of commodities now and twelve or thirteen years ago, affects this country itself.

In the first place, it is clear, as already stated incidentally, that all persons having fixed incomes payable in gold have gained enormously of late years.

All the necessaries of life—bread, butter, eggs, sugar, bacon, tea, coffee, clothing, the metals worked and unworked, and even fresh meat and milk—are from 20 to 75 per cent. cheaper than they were. Thus the interest on the National Debt, say £28,000,000, and the income from the railways, say £33,000,000, have a purchasing power of at least £40,000,000 and £48,000,000 respectively, compared with what they had previously to the great fall in prices. The same is of course true of interest on mortgages, and all other incomes receivable in gold. But the great bulk of these incomes, from investment, are paid to the non-producing classes; so great a proportion, indeed, that what is received by the workers is a neglectable quantity. Now what does this really mean? It means that, taking the two above instances only, the actual weight of the National Debt and the railway monopoly upon the community has increased 40 per cent., as measured in commodities, assuming that the purchasing power of gold has increased 40 per cent. with reference to the majority of commodities; and this may be taken as a reasonable average if wholesale prices are reckoned. If retail prices have not fallen in the same degree, then the large shopkeepers have pocketed the difference, and they, again, are a non-producing class. Consequently, the effect of the fall in prices is to increase the relative wealth and influence of the rent and interest-receiving minority.

Again, it is undoubted that a constantly descending scale of prices, though in one way it strengthens the capitalist class, is not favourable to capitalist enterprise, as distinguished even from mere inflation. In agriculture, for instance, farmers who have not already lost their capital are afraid to make improvements, to buy store beasts, or to launch out in any direction, because the prices they may get for their produce, when grown, and their beasts, when fattened, may not repay them for their original outlay, leaving aside profit altogether. The workers also, though the half-a-crown and shilling buy in England as an eighth, and a twentieth of a pound respectively, and not as 1*s.* 8*d.* and 8*d.*, which they would if their intrinsic value determined their purchasing power,—though the workers who use this token coinage which they receive in wages are not injured directly, I say, and receive the benefit of the low prices of the necessaries of life, yet they are injured indirectly, by the stagnation of trade and the growing uncertainty of their position.

It will be seen that it is not the deficiency of gold *as currency* which occasions all this disturbance, but the appreciation of gold as a *standard of value*, and therefore as the regulator of prices, which does the mischief, in so far as mischief is done.

There are those who argue that all is more than repaid to us by the low prices of raw material for our manufactures and of our food, which enable our capitalists to undersell the capitalists of other countries. I have shown, however, that the increased drain, owing to the appreciation of gold, impoverishes some of our best customers in India; it certainly is one of the causes of the heavy pressure of rents in Ireland, in spite of the statutory reductions; it unquestionably helps to increase the distress of our own agriculturists; and I cannot understand how any such action which impoverishes our fellow-subjects, by constant alterations in prices, due to the increased cost of production of gold, can in the long run be of advantage to ourselves. That this should be so is contrary not only to common-sense, but to the whole argument of the *laissez-faire* school to which the more vehement gold advocates belong.

In conclusion, therefore, it would seem that, assuming it to be impossible to make any other arrangement, which is certainly not yet proved, it would be better to monetise silver and demonetise gold all the world over, than to continue a system which enhances the weight of indebtedness and taxation at the expense of the producing classes, not only in India, but in all countries where the principal and interest of indebtedness are payable in gold. At the same time, no change in the currency or lowering of the standard of value—raising of prices, that is—will affect the deep economical difficulties which underlie all questions relating to gold as currency, as a standard of value, or as payment for indebtedness; these difficulties being due, as they are, to the capitalist system of production and the national debts which have accompanied and assisted its growth.

Meanwhile, as we debate, India, at any rate, is being reduced to bankruptcy with ever-increasing rapidity.